Every Blessing
JACOB + Kathleen

BELFAST'S BROWN SQUARE

HIDDEN GOLD

Kathleen McKee
with Jack McKee

"The greatest legacy one can pass on to children is
not money or other material things accumulated
in one's life, but rather a legacy of character and faith."

Billy Graham

(Paraphrased)

HIDDEN GOLD

ISBN: 978-1-8384838-4-5

All Scriptures quoted are taken from THE HOLY BIBLE, NEW INTERNATIONAL VERSION®, NIV® Copyright © 1973, 1978, 1984, 2011 by Biblica, Inc.® Used by permission. All rights reserved worldwide.

Published by
Maurice Wylie Media
Your Inspirational Publisher

Front cover: Argyle Street, Shankill Road, not far from Brown Square. Little girl on bike is Sandra Fitzgerald, now Sandra Muir who now lives in Scotland. Photo by Mr Brian Seed, permission granted.

All profits from this book will be donated to Hobby Horse Playgroup

For more information visit
www.MauriceWylieMedia.com

Contents

Endorsements

"I first came into contact with Kathleen McKee in 1991, although I knew of the work both she and Jack were attempting to do in the Greater Shankill area. I knew of them both but came to meet Kathleen through her work with the children of the Greater Shankill area. At the time I met Kathleen, I was managing a project called 'Cairnmartin Wood Products'. The project made play furniture for Nurseries, Parent and Toddler groups etc. Kathleen came to see our products and an instant bond was formed between us. She was determined to try and make a better future for 'Her Children' as she described them. In the following years, and struggling against the odds, Kathleen became more ambitious in relation to her work and she never lost 'Her Vision' for the children. I am very pleased to write this endorsement about this part of the early-years history, and a woman who never gave up."

Baroness May Blood MBE, Belfast, Northern Ireland.

"I have known Kathleen for almost 30 years in her role as Playgroup Leader in Hobby Horse Playgroup. Kathleen always struck me as one of the kindest, most humble, unassuming people I had ever met and yet behind that quiet exterior was a woman of steely courage who was not afraid to push the boundaries in terms of creating inclusive quality early years experiences in one of the most divided and polarised communities in Northern Ireland.

Kathleen and Hobby Horse were one of the first playgroups in Northern Ireland to implement the evidence-based Media Initiative Respecting Difference Programme, introducing young children and their families to celebrate a strong sense of their own unionist, loyalist identities, while also celebrating and respecting nationalist, republican culture.

I have been privileged to know Kathleen, and I wish her a long and happy retirement."

Dr Siobhan Fitzpatrick MBE CEO of Early Years NI. Belfast, Northern Ireland.

"I met Kathleen (known to us as Kathy) in 1975. Since then, we have been great friends. Kathleen had a great heart for children and would often be seen leading children from her area and meeting up with our friend Jean, who would be leading children from another part of the Shankill on their way to the children's meeting, "Sunshine Corner", at church. They would be met by one of the men from the church holding a lollipop sign to assist them across the main road and into the church. It was always amazing to see those children arriving at church.

When Kathleen had told us that she was going to Bible College with Jackie, I was delighted but also challenged, as I knew I was going to be the one to fill her shoes at Sunshine Corner. I had big shoes to fill because Kathleen loved those children, and they loved her; it wasn't hard to love her. She was just lovely, with her lovely smile and selfless ways, always thinking of others, a wonderful and loving person, and since leaving us for Bible College, and having been in ministry with Jack for many years, she has never changed from being that loving, selfless person."

Margaret McCurley (A personal friend), Belfast Northern Ireland.

Our Thankfulness

I first met Kathleen when my son attended Hobby Horse Playgroup in 1997. After a few weeks of my son attending, I was asked by Kathleen if I would be able to work temporarily at Hobby Horse to cover Lorraine's maternity leave. I was able and happy to do so, which is when I began to get to know Kathleen.

After a few weeks of working within Hobby Horse, I realised that this was what I wanted to do as a profession. Kathleen encouraged me to progress my learning and received funding for me to complete my Diplomas and start my journey in the childcare profession. Watching Kathleen with the children, her kind and caring nature always shone through. The children related to this and always loved to engage with her, often fighting over a seat to be next to her.

Kathleen was always there for me for guidance, not only in my profession but also in my private life, becoming a very dear friend. I could always rely on her and confide in her for advice, and she was always willing to help. Over the years, I have witnessed Kathleen help families in different circumstances and situations, both within and outside of Hobby Horse, from gifting money to paying for electricity and providing food parcels when a family was in need. Nothing was ever any trouble to her when it came to helping others.

I have worked alongside Kathleen for over 20 years, and everyday it's been a pleasure to come to work. We have not only been a team of employees, but to Kathleen we were like family.

Kathleen has taught me what a childcare worker should be. Today, after all these years, I see the children look at me the way that children looked at Kathleen, which is down to everything Kathleen taught me, and I know as well as the kiddies of Hobby Horse that I had the best teacher. Thank you, Kathleen.

Maureen Mann, Manager of Hobby Horse Playgroup.

In 1994, I attended New Life Fellowship where I first met Kathleen. At that first meeting, I didn't realise how she would influence me both spiritually, personally and professionally. I began attending the mothers and toddlers with my daughter, who was two at the time. Kathleen then asked if I would consider taking the mother and toddlers on a casual basis. As I was unemployed at that time, this was a great opportunity for me, as it was something I could get involved with, and I could also bring my daughter along with me. This gave us both an opportunity to get out and mix with other young mums and children.

When my daughter started school, Kathleen then asked me if I would be interested in doing a childcare course. I jumped at the chance. It meant going to class one day a week and doing a placement in Hobby Horse Playgroup. There were also two other girls doing this course with me that Kathleen had also encouraged to progress in their further education (Wendy and Amanda). It was while doing this I really decided that this was what I wanted to do as a profession. Kathleen has been my mentor throughout this professional journey, firstly employing me and giving me the opportunity to do a job that I absolutely adore. She worked hard to encourage me to do my Level 3 and Level 5 in Childcare, besides securing the funding to pay for them both, which is something I could never have afforded to do myself. Kathleen mentored and helped me any way she could throughout the process, and over the past 23 years that I have worked in Hobby Horse, she has always encouraged me to do courses to improve my professional knowledge.

Kathleen has also always been there for me personally. She has helped me get through many situations in my life that I felt I had nowhere and no one to turn to. She has always encouraged me to keep looking forward, put my trust in God and that nothing is too big that can't be fixed. She really has been an inspiration to me, always putting others first and showing such a caring and gentle nature. I have been truly blessed to have her in my life, not only in a professional capacity, but as a friend.

Lorraine Barr, Senior Supervisor Hobby Horse Playgroup.

I don't know what to say about Kathleen that others don't already know. She is a true lady and has always been a friend, not just the Leader of Hobby Horse. I have known her for 30 years. During this time, she has always been there to talk to and to help whenever possible. She has helped me many times, just being able to talk to her. In all these years I have known her, she has never changed a bit. I will always remember the laughs and the chats. I love her to bits.

Sandra Selby, (children attended Hobby Horse Playgroup.)

I was one of the first children to attend Hobby Horse when it started in the old Stadium. When I became a mother, there was never a doubt in my mind that I wanted my child to have the same experience with Kathleen and with Hobby Horse. Our whole family has gone to Hobby Horse from when it was in the Stadium, and when it moved to Townsend Street, when it moved to the old Elim Church and then to the Presbyterian Church, and then when it moved to its present location in City Life Centre, Northumberland Street. We all got to experience the kind of nurturing environment created by Kathleen. I would not have changed it for the world.

Amy Wamie

Dedication

As one who has fought to achieve the fulfilment of her dreams, I want to dedicate this book to those who likewise have had to fight to see their dreams fulfilled, and especially to those who fought for their very lives, although sadly some lost that fight, two of whom were precious children, Madison Bothwell and Dempsey Ballantyne who left us all too soon and left such a mark in our hearts and in the hearts of many others.

Four-year-old Madison Bothwell attended Hobby Horse Playgroup for his pre-school year, but sadly lost his young life in a fire alongside his father and his grandmother, the result of a tragic accident at home.

Dempsey Ballantyne attended *New Life City Church* along with her mum, Lynn McInally. Sadly, after a three-year battle against cancer, Dempsey lost her young life when she was only eight years of age.

I want to also give a special mention to all those who have stood by us during the past 30 years. Ever since I was a teenager, I have worked with children and families throughout the Shankill community in Belfast. I began as a volunteer helper in a children's outreach in a local church that I refer to later, which led ultimately to the launch of Hobby Horse Playgroup in September 1989. It started out with 16 children in a little back room but later developed to become Hobby Horse Family Project that today includes our daily pre-school Playgroup, our after-school Butterfly Club for children with additional needs, mainly autism, and our Parents & Toddlers Group, besides offering additional support to parents and the broader family. We could not have done this without the original support of New Life City Church and of Stadium Projects (now called City Life Projects), and would never have got to where we are today without the amazing support of the Department for Communities, Social Services, NIPPA and Early Years, TBF Thompson Trust, and other funders.

Last and surely not least, I want to mention our amazing staff, especially two very special people who became two amazing friends, Maureen Mann and Lorraine Barr, but also our volunteers, our Management Team, and every child who has been part of the incredible Hobby Horse journey.

I love you all!

Kathleen McKee

Foreword

As I sat in the church café with Kathleen, I was pondering over the title of this book, and reflecting on the people from our old community of Brown Square, when suddenly I heard the words, "These people are like hidden gold." Instantly I knew those words reflected the content of this book and especially the person, the nature and the character of Kathleen McKee.

I certainly know that I could not have done what I've done in life and in ministry without having alongside me the perfect match of a wife and partner who possessed the God-given qualities of a lioness; qualities that I was always aware of, but were only seen by others when the situation caused those qualities to rise and come to the fore.

Kathleen might well have been dove-like in her public demeanour, but whenever the circumstances called for it, and believe me there were many such circumstances, she became as brave as any lioness that stands in defence of those in its care. Whether it was for her church family, her immediate family, or for those whom God had entrusted to her, she was the lioness who would stand between them and whatever it was that sought to threaten them, whether from terrorism, ill health, or from personal or community deprivation. Yet, at the same time she was a loving homemaker, a caring mother, and much more than a wife; a partner, a soul mate and my forever friend.

It has been such an amazing privilege to not only be the husband of Kathleen, but to literally do life with her; and what a life! Yes, we've had our trials, and there've been many, with the latest being that in recent years Kathleen has been struggling with illness, which is referenced at the end of this book. It is this illness that has led to the writing of this book that we have worked on together for almost two years; going back and forth when she could recall and share memories to record the journey.

These are her stories, reflecting her life and her faith, but shared and written with my help, as I narrate and introduce Kathleen throughout.

Kathleen, you're one in a million. I'm honoured to walk with you.

Jack McKee MBE

Chapter 1

Brown Square Millionaires

Being a Pastor's wife was not something that Kathleen had dreamed of ever being or even wanted to be. In fact, when I first mentioned the idea of Bible College and of becoming a Pastor, which was during the first year of our married life, her immediate reaction was to reject such an idea. She did so for quite a while, until a very special moment when God spoke to her heart in such a way that in her own words she said, "God spoke so clearly to me one night that I was left in no doubt that God was calling us to Bible College, and that one day I would serve alongside Jackie in full-time pastoral ministry". She has now done so for over forty years; and still counting.

Kathleen was often the person in the background, and has always been affectionately known as "Pastor Jack's wife." This was not as a position of servitude, but one of working in partnership alongside her husband, and of doing so in the heart of one of Northern Ireland's most notorious political and religious conflict zones, where she witnessed and experienced much more than any woman should ever have had to endure.

However, there were times when Kathleen almost never did make it to the dizzy heights of being a Pastor's wife. For example, there was the night when death came knocking on her door; when it almost took her life and with it her future family not yet born, not to mention her lifelong ministry through which God enabled her in her own quiet and determined way to touch and help many who were living in one of the worst-affected areas of 'The Troubles' in Northern Ireland. Yet, in a strange way, it was a night and an unforgettable moment that helped prepare her for other dangerous and challenging situations when death would again come knocking at the door of family members, friends, neighbours and church members, and would also come knocking again at the door of our family home.

A Girl from the Backstreets

Kathleen was born and raised in the backstreets of Belfast at the bottom of the Shankill Road in an area known as Brown Square. It was a small community where people had very little in terms of material wealth, but what they did have, they shared. And yet regardless of their financial and material lack, the people in this rundown slum had enough self-belief to call themselves Brown Square Millionaires. In fact, they even sang a song about their perceived millionaire status, although the song was more about the Rowdy Girls' Dart Team in Brown Square, proudly boasting of their success in throwing darts, singing about "making money fly and kissing boys as they went by;" but it seemed like everyone within that little community was referred to collectively as "The Brown Square Millionaires". They were rich in hope, humour and hospitality, and Kathleen was one of those "millionaires" whose wealth was not based on money, but on having the kind of friends and family that money couldn't buy.

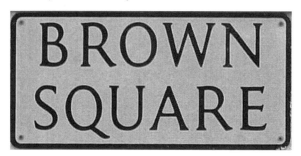

Brown Square street sign

Most adults living in Brown Square were either unemployed or worked in low paid labouring jobs. Most of these were in Hall's Brush Factory or in Hicks Bullick spinning mill, both of which were located within Brown Square itself, although Kathleen's father, Geordie McDermott, worked as a mechanic for the RAF in Aldergrove Airport just outside Belfast. Her mother, Bell McDermott, worked from home for a Jewish Money-Lender who gave loans to the "Millionaires" in Brown Square. However, although her parents were making more income than most others in Brown Square, it didn't change the fact that like everyone else within our little community they also lived in a very small house where the living room was called the kitchen, and where instead of a kitchen we had a scullery, and inside the scullery was a large white jaw box ("Belfast sink"), which was just called "the kitchen sink". Talk about confusion! Besides this, there was no inside bathroom or toilet, but a toilet located in the backyard, and a tin bath hanging proudly on a six-inch (15cms) nail on the yard wall that was taken down once a week, filled with warm water, and in you got for your weekly bath; although for some it was monthly!

Sitting at the heart of our community was Brown Square Primary School. It seemed like everything radiated from the school like spokes from the hub of a wheel that extended out to Hall's Brush Factory, Hicks Bullick Spinning Mill and three churches, the Elim Pentecostal Church in Melbourne Street (often referred with great affection as the wee Elim), the Presbyterian Church in Townsend Street, and St. Stephen's Church of Ireland in Millfield. Then there were several corner shops that had as much stolen from them as what was bought from them, with the most famous being Lizzie Adair's at the corner of Sackville Street opposite the Primary School. It was not only the most famous shop in the Square due to its location, but it was also the most robbed; not that Kathleen ever stole from it, she was too nice a person, but the guy she married did; although very much in his pre-pastor days!

Melbourne Street Elim Church

Kathleen and I would often reflect on those days, when in some weird way I would take delight in sharing with her how I would've gone into Lizzie Adair's and asked for a quarter pound of cheese, knowing that Lizzie would have to go to the back of the shop to slice and weigh it, so that by the time she came back with the cheese, I would have been up and over the other side of the counter and back again with cigarettes and sweets stuffed in my pockets. We've often wondered how poor old Lizzie and other shop owners managed to survive, but survive they did!

Then of course there were the pubs, with the main one being the Coronation Bar at the corner of Wilson Street and Sackville Street: a bar whose owners were Catholics, and yet virtually all the customers were Protestants.

Kathleen knew that the back wall of the Coronation Bar connected with the yard wall of my house, and so part of our Brown Square reflections includes the time I climbed the yard wall and broke into the pub and stole alcohol and cigarettes. This is the person who would one day become a pastor, with Kathleen as his wife, and here he was stealing from Lizzie Adair's and breaking into the Coronation Bar; but obviously all prior to my relationship with Kathleen and all before becoming a Christian, never mind a pastor!

Kathleen's early reflections

For this book, I asked Kathleen to share some of her early memories of what it was like being raised and living in Brown Square. She shared the following:

"My early memories of childhood in Brown Square are of playing street games, which is something you don't see these days. It was normal that after school you would meet your friends in the street, and there you'd stay until you were called into the house for your dinner. Then after dinner, you'd go back outside to play again where you'd stay until you were called in again at bedtime. Besides tying a rope around an old gas lamppost to make a swing, I loved playing street games like hopscotch, skipping, jacks, queenio, kick the tin, rallyo, hunts, and many other outdoor games that kept us occupied and kept us out of trouble; unless we got drawn into something more *mischievous* like knock the door and run away! It was all innocent fun with my friends in the streets.

"Not many of us had bicycles in Brown Square, although a few did. Jackie would often borrow a bike from Andy Calderwood, who loaned it to him because he went to the bookies for him, or he would rent a bike for a few pennies from a man in Coates Street. I was one of the lucky ones, because I did have my own bike, although when I was younger, I had a tricycle, which was easier to ride and was more for a girl than a boy. I used to let a friend stand on the bar at the back, so I usually had company."

Kathleen mentions Andy Calderwood. He was one of nine brothers and two sisters. They were Brown Square's most renown family. One of them was married to my mum's sister Nellie, Tommy (Mousey) Calderwood, which made him my uncle and meant I was connected to the Calderwoods, and I was happy with that!

7 of the 9 Calderwood brothers at their sister's wedding at St. Stephen's Church

'Doughboy' Calderwood (right on previous photo) carries bomb from van to waste ground [1]

The previous comments from Kathleen inspired me to write the following:

SUNNY BROWN SQUARE

Skipping ropes and lamppost swings
A piece of chalk and simple things
An old leather ball we'd kick down the street
With often no boots to put on our feet
For we lived on a wing and a prayer
Yet we loved it there in sunny Brown Square

Some brought spuds and some brought beef
Yet what we made was beyond belief
A pot of stew that could feed a troop
Was more than enough and was better than soup
For we lived life on a wing and a prayer
But we loved it there in sunny Brown Square

(Jack McKee)

1 From Francis Higgins' book: Religion, Riots & Rebels

Some of the Brown Square Corner Boys sitting outside the Primary School

Kathleen continues with her early day memories of Brown Square that included how she and I met and started dating. She shares the following:

"When I was only 15, I was in my final year at Everton Girls' School. Unknown to me, Jackie was planning to ask me out on our first date. Even though I knew him and had seen him in church, it was my good friend Jean Nelson that said to me on the school bus, "Jackie McKee wants to know if you'll go out with him." Well, in an instant, it was like I heard the singing of angels accompanied by heavenly music; which is what Jackie likes to believe, but with a nervous laughter I said to Jean, "Yes, I'll go out with him." Two nights later, we met for our first date. He took me to the local fish and chip shop, Lizzie Brady's in Cargill Street, where together we shared a plate of chips with two forks, and had a small glass of coke each (Coca Cola that is). Jackie paid for the lavish meal with money he'd borrowed from his dad. It was certainly not a posh meal, but it was nonetheless romantic and was the start of our relationship that was to lead to a lifelong marriage, three children and seven grandchildren, and, although I didn't know it at the time, it was also the first step to becoming the wife of a pastor."

Tough times get tougher

So, Kathleen and I had hit it off, although we were not really strangers. My mum was one of Kathleen's mum's clients who had taken out a loan from the Jewish Money Lender. This meant I would often go to Kathleen's home with money from my mum to pay off some of the loan or sometimes to ask for more money. In fact, it was usually the latter, which always put a smile on the Money Lender's face! However, more importantly, we had both become committed Christians prior to our first date. We both attended the same local Elim Church in Brown Square, and went to the same youth group. It was there we really started to get to know each other, encouraged by some of our youth leaders who believed they were doing God's work by doing a bit of matchmaking. So, when I asked Kathleen out on a date, we already knew each other; but it was still unexpected by her, and a pleasant surprise on my part when she said, "Yes".

Barricade between Catholic Coates Street and Protestant Brown's Square. The soldier is standing between Jackie's home and his Granny Hammond's home.

In spite of the fact that life was tough in Brown Square, I have to say that for Kathleen and me, life was good. We really were two teenagers in love, but we had no idea where our relationship would go, or where the journey we were now on would take us. Before Kathleen had finished her last year in school, I had got my very first job in the local brush factory, which meant that whenever we went back to the local chip shop, I was able to buy a plate of chips for each of us, instead of just one with two forks, so things were really looking up for us!

However, not long after our first date, 'The Troubles' in Northern Ireland broke out between Protestants and Catholics. Although it had started 80 miles north of Belfast, in the city of Derry/Londonderry, within 24 hours it had spread to our little community in Brown Square to such an extent that it became one of the main battle areas of the early days of what's now referred to throughout the world as 'The Troubles'.

Barricades were quickly erected between the warring communities, including Brown Square and our neighbouring Catholic communities. Both Kathleen's home and my home were right next to two barricades, but they were not high enough or strong enough to prevent the people from getting at each other from either side, which they did repeatedly. Sadly, things had changed forever.

Brown Square would never be the same as street fighting and rioting became a daily and nightly activity, with homes being burned and destroyed and with people being shot and killed. The streets that would normally smell of bacon or fish being fried, now reeked with the constant smell of smoke from burning buildings, and the normally quiet week-nights were disturbed with the constant sound of gunfire, grenades and rioting.

Men, old and young, were suddenly thrust onto the streets as vigilantes, where they would patrol each night in a joint endeavour to protect our little community and to warn of any attack or even the threat of one. I was only 17 at the time, but I was old enough to be a vigilante, and so with other men I would spend many nights walking the streets or standing at street corners around an open fire. Often after leaving Kathleen home, and after a few goodnight kisses, I would take my place on the street or at the barricades alongside some of our friends and neighbours.

Most nights were fine insofar as we felt safe in each other's company, but then there were nights that were anything but fine, when serious rioting broke out between us Protestants in Brown Square, and our neighbouring Catholics in the Coates Street and Divis Street area. These riots always resulted in serious damage being done on both sides. People were hurt quite badly, some being injured by bricks that were often thrown by those at the back of their own crowd, who couldn't throw to save their lives. No one really knew what to expect. On reflecting on those nights, Kathleen shares the following:

"I remember one night when, not long after Jackie had left me home, someone came rushing into our home screaming, "Jackie's been hurt." I froze with fear, but then ran out to the street, not knowing what had happened. I saw an ambulance and feared the worst. Someone then told me that Jackie was inside the ambulance, which made me even more concerned. They wouldn't let me join him, but assured me he would be okay. Then after about 30 minutes of further medical treatment, and with some more tears on my part, Jackie was finally brought out of the ambulance and all was well."

Soldier looking towards Primary School and Lizzie Adair's corner shop, top right.

From the frying pan into the fire

Sadly, those early nights and weeks of violence not only continued, but got worse with every passing day and night. Brown Square continued to be one of those communities that bore the brunt of the conflict; a conflict that some called a war, but a brutal and dirty war. Life in Brown Square became much more challenging than ever it was, and it came as no surprise when just two years into the conflict, Brown Square succumbed to a government redevelopment plan. In reality, it was much more like a resettlement plan: a plan that resulted in most of our old neighbourhood being demolished, leading to almost all of us having to leave our old homes with their sculleries and outside toilets, and moving into new homes in a new housing development at the bottom end of the Shankill Road. This was an area called Denmark Street; an area that was to become one of the most infamous and deadly in Northern Ireland's conflict. Brown Square was hot and fearsome at times, but Denmark Street would later become an inferno.

The new houses in Denmark Street were certainly much better than the rat and cockroach infested houses in Brown Square, plus the fact that they all had front and back gardens, something we never had in Brown Square! They also had indoor bathrooms with an indoor bath and toilet, plus a kitchen that really was a kitchen and a proper living room where the entire family could fit in. We could watch television together in the same room, never mind being able to fit into the same house.

However, the move was very much like "out of the frying pan and into the fire," because Denmark Street was destined to become greatly impacted by the conflict. Some of its new residents from Brown Square would become victims to the violence, and some would pay the ultimate price with their lives being tragically and brutally taken from them. No one had a crystal ball; ouija boards and tea leaves yes, but not a crystal ball; and so, we had no idea of what lay ahead. But even if we did, we could not stop what the Housing Executive called "progress" and could not prevent what was happening to Brown Square and its people. The writing was on the wall. Brown Square, as we knew it, was about to go. The people were going and, regardless of all the promises, they would not be back.

Maryanne Hammond (Jackie's granny) in her new Denmark Street home, her two daughters (Nellie & Maggie – Jackie's mum) at their old home in Brown Square

Accepting the inevitable, someone, or some family, had to be the first to leave the old Brown Square and be the first to make the move into the new homes in Denmark Street. For some unknown reason, Kathleen's mum and dad, George and Bell McDermott, along with Kathleen and her brother Bill, were chosen to be the first family to make the move. So, if anyone wants to know who the first family was to move into the new houses in Denmark Street, it was the McDermotts! Others would make the move in the weeks that followed, including my parents, my three brothers, Sammy, Tommy and Alcwyn, and of course me.

However, until we made the actual move to Denmark Street, I would walk Kathleen to her new home at the end of each night, and would then make my way on foot back to what was still our home in Brown Square. Although, not without locking what was a makeshift workman's gate that had been erected by the builders at the entrance of the new Denmark Street development, which at that time was still very much a building site.

The reason for the gate being in place was that the new development was at a major interface between Protestant Denmark Street and Catholic Antrim Road, and so each night I would lock Kathleen and her family in as the only family that lived in Denmark Street at that time. Kathleen would stand at her door and watch me leave, watching as I made my way back to Brown Square, knowing it would not only be a lonely walk, but a dangerous one. This was 1971 when it was anything but safe to be on the streets alone. There were no mobile phones, and we had no house phones, and so Kathleen had no idea if I made it safely back home, which meant living on her nerves until she saw or heard that everything was okay. Those were days when the phrase, "No news is good news" really meant something, whether it was Kathleen and her family being on their own in Denmark Street, or it was me going through that same routine each night, thankful to God for His hand upon us as families and as individuals. Eventually we moved into our new home just three doors from Kathleen's in Denmark Street.

Kathleen's parents, George & Bell McDermott in their new Denmark Street home during later renovations

But whether it was Brown Square or Denmark Street, 'The Troubles' in Belfast and across Northern Ireland were getting worse. Vigilante groups were being replaced by Paramilitary Groups that soon became heavily armed terrorist organisations, fully embedded on both sides of the divide. In time they would not only inflict pain and death on "the other side," but would cause pain and death within their respective communities that they had vowed to defend and protect. This they did for the purpose of community control and domination. In turn, that was to lead to organised crime, with all the social evils that accompany it.

Kathleen shares the following regarding her early working years:

"When Jackie and I moved into our new homes in Denmark Street, I'd been working as a Stitcher in the Ladybird sewing factory for at least two years, having left school at the age of 15. My main job was stitching collars onto men's shirts. I loved it there and made many good friends, one of them being Florrie Orr. Even though she was a bit older than me, I was really drawn to her because Florrie was also a Christian and was a big help and encouragement to me as a young Christian. One day, Florrie shared with us that she was going out with a man called Jimmy Stewart. We were all excited for her. Florrie was a lovely girl and Jimmy was a nice Christian man. But sadly, within two short months of their first date, Jimmy was out shopping on a Saturday afternoon (4th March, 1972) when he called into the Abercorn Restaurant in Belfast for a coffee. Tragically, within minutes, Jimmy's life was to change forever as an IRA bomb ripped through the premises, killing two young Catholic girls, and injuring over 100 from across Belfast and beyond, both Protestant and Catholic. Jimmy was one of those victims. As the bomb exploded, it ripped off both his legs in an instant.

"Thanks to the quick response of the emergency services, Jimmy's life was saved, but it would never be the same. Knowing this, he decided to end his relationship with Florrie. He told her to leave him and to forget about him, but Florrie made it clear that she never had any intention of turning her back on him, saying it was the Lord who brought them together. With Florrie's unwavering devotion and with the help of the medical profession, within a year Jimmy was walking again with the aid of artificial limbs. Two and a half years after the bombing, Jimmy and Florrie married in October 1974 in the Welcome Church within the Shankill community. They were later to be blessed with two boys, Paul and Stephen. We might have left Brown Square behind, but we hadn't left 'The Troubles' there."

Chapter 2
The Soldier's Wife

Kathleen referred to Jimmy Stewart's brush with death, which came during the third year of the conflict and during one of the darkest periods of 'The Troubles'; a time when paramilitary groups on both sides of the divide were getting stronger in terms of firepower and were growing in terms of manpower. Kathleen and I watched as our friends and family members joined these paramilitary groups within the Protestant community. This led to our having conversations about our response to what was going on, especially with my family, but we both knew that whatever decision I would make, would have an impact on her life and our future relationship.

We both knew that being a vigilante was one thing, and I was happy doing that with the men in our community, men I knew and trusted, but to sign up to what was clearly a terrorist organisation was something we both knew I could not do as a committed Christian. Yet, we also knew that I could not just retreat into the house and do nothing. We both agreed that I needed to do something, and so with Kathleen's blessing and approval, wrapped up in a lot of concern, I decided to do things legally by joining the British Army. I became a soldier in the Ulster Defence Regiment (UDR) in February 1972. The UDR was a newly formed Regiment in the British Army based within Northern Ireland, and consisted of 10,000 part-time and full-time soldiers. I was to serve three years part-time and then full-time for another three years.

In thinking back to those early days in the UDR, Kathleen shared the following: "When I worked in the Ladybird with Florrie, and before the Abercorn bombing, I remember that some of us from the Ladybird would often walk home together along the Crumlin Road, and in doing so, would pass by the main prison in Northern Ireland, the Crumlin Road Jail. Several times while passing the prison, I would hear a whistle coming from the direction of the prison, and I would sometimes hear my name being called out. It was Jackie sitting in the prison sanger, providing security for the prison, which at that time held several hundred paramilitary prisoners from both sides of the conflict. Jackie would be looking out over the Crumlin Road, while also keeping an eye on what was happening inside the prison. So, I knew it helped brighten his day when he saw me walking past on my way home."

Early fears as a young wife

While in the UDR, most of my time on duty was spent protecting key installations such as the gasworks and power stations, but I would also spend time on foot patrol through the streets of North Belfast or driving an armour-protected Land Rover. I would often share stories with Kathleen of things that had happened while on duty. I didn't tell her everything, but I had no idea that what little I did share was having such an impact on her and that she carried hidden fears every time I was out. Kathleen shares the following:

"At times Jackie's stories really did frighten me, but at other times I was encouraged to know that he and his friends were saving lives. Some of his stories made me wonder if he might not come home the next time he was out on duty. At times I would lie awake at night wondering where he was, hoping and praying he was okay, but always breathing a sigh of relief when I heard the car stop outside the front of our home, because only then did I know he was safe.

"The fear I felt was increased greatly when he and some of his friends were told by the police that when they raided the home of a well-known IRA terrorist in the Ardoyne area of North Belfast, among other things they found, was a list of names of security members who were being targeted by the IRA. We were told that Jackie's name was on that list. This changed how we lived, and led to Jackie being armed when he was off duty. He would carry a personal firearm everywhere he went. He brought it to church with him and even brought it to bed and put it under his pillow because people were being shot dead in their own bedrooms.

"Several months after we received this warning, Jackie and I were married, on 4th November 1972. Before that amazing day in our lives, we went through one of the darkest periods of 'The Troubles' with many other bombings, shootings and deaths. It was just such a horrible time, even for some of our friends and neighbours who had moved from Brown Square and were now living in their new homes in Denmark Street. Despite all the trouble we had experienced and witnessed in Brown Square, I don't ever remember any funerals taking place there that were directly related to 'The Troubles', but Denmark Street was a different story.

Jimmy and Florrie Stewart.
Jimmy lost both his legs in the IRA bombing of
the Abercorn Restaurant

"One of the first of our friends and neighbours from Brown Square to be murdered was Bobby McComb. I had known Bobby quite well. In fact, our families were connected, as were most of the families in Brown Square. He and his family had made the move to Denmark Street several weeks after us. Bobby had attended the same school and the same Sunday school that Jackie and I had both gone to, and would often have been seen playing football on the street along with Jackie and some of their other friends. Bobby was much quieter than most of the young men of his age in Brown Square. I had never seen him involved in a fight, even though there were many fights in Brown Square, and I had never known him to be in any kind of trouble. His sister Violet shared with me that Bobby would often say to her, "Never bring up your children to hate," and thankfully, regardless of all the tragedies she has gone through in her life, Violet honoured Bobby's words. I've had the joy and the pleasure of sitting next to Violet in church on Sunday mornings for many years, but not many know the pain she has experienced due to the murder of her brother Bobby and the shooting of her husband Sammy. I'll let Jackie share the story from here."

Death came knocking on Denmark Street

While many of our friends were joining paramilitary organisations, Bobby and I chose not to do so, but we chose to join the UDR. When a reporter asked him why he joined the UDR, Bobby replied by saying that he believed he could make a difference. Some might laugh and sneer, but Bobby McComb really did believe he could help bring an end to the violence in Northern Ireland. He had no idea he would soon be one of the early victims of the conflict he hoped he could help end.

On Saturday 22nd July 1972, just a few months before Kathleen and I were married, Bobby had arranged to go out with his brother Tommy along with Violet's husband Sammy. Well at least, that was the plan. But Sammy got detained and never made it on time to meet with them, so Bobby and Tommy went off to a local bar where they were met by their brother Davy who was one of my best friends while growing up in Brown Square. Davy is now living in Canada, where he's been for many years. Anyway, Bobby left the bar along with a young woman he had met in the bar that night. Leaving his brothers Tommy and Davy back in the bar, he walked a short distance to the young woman's home. He left her at her front door and then began walking alone along the dark streets in search of a taxi to take him back to Denmark Street.

As he walked along a street within the Shankill community where he should have been safe, Bobby was picked up, but sadly not by a taxi. He was picked up by an IRA murder squad who had been driving through the Shankill looking for an unsuspecting victim. Anyone would do, but Bobby just happened to be on the street that night, alone and unarmed. The following morning, Bobby's blindfolded body was found not far from his Denmark Street home. He had been severely tortured; badly beaten, bones broken, cigarette burns on his face, his chest burned with a hot steam-iron, and had the shape of a cross burned into his back, and with the letters 'IRA' branded next to the cross. There were other marks on his body that showed he had been dragged over rough ground, and then eventually shot in the head. The guilt of Bobby's murder, like many others in Northern Ireland, is laid firmly on the shoulders of those who carried out the brutal act and on the one who finally pulled the trigger, but also on those who heard the screams and the shots being fired and who still to this day remain silent.

Bobby McComb was not only a neighbour; he was one of our friends. In fact, Bobby was the first of our friends from Brown Square and the first from our new Denmark Street homes to fall victim to the IRA murdering campaign. Sadly, he would not be the last, nor would his death be the end of the pain for the McComb family, especially his sister Violet. She sits next to Kathleen, and Kathleen's two sisters Marie and Sally, in church on Sunday mornings. Having lost her brother Bobby, Violet would later watch her husband Sammy fight for his life after two members of the Irish National Liberation Army (INLA) burst into his home in Denmark Street and shot him five times, hitting him in the back and severing his spinal cord. He survived the murder attempt, but was left paralysed from the waist down. For Sammy and Violet Miller, life would never be the same. Sammy spent twelve days on life support, five weeks in intensive care, seven months in hospital, and three years undergoing numerous operations, and then spent the rest of his life in a wheelchair. He passed away several years later. Violet has carried the pain of such loss for many years and to this very day.

Kathleen says, "I am honoured that Violet and I have been able to sit alongside each other in church on Sunday mornings. I know she carries the memories of several people she has loved and lost in tragic circumstances, including more recently her daughter Cathy, a mother of five children who lost her life to a brain tumour. Yet, Violet continues through such pain to hold on to her faith as she lives daily with the knowledge and the hope that someday she will meet her loved ones again. I am not only glad that we were neighbours in Brown Square and Denmark Street, but I'm also honoured to call her a friend".

Wedding Bells in Denmark Street

1971 and 1972 were extremely difficult years for many reasons, but 1972 was to end on a much happier note because that was the year Kathleen and I had planned to marry. And marry we did on the 4th November, even though we had faced situations that could have prevented us from making it to the altar. I think I'm right in saying that we were the first couple to be married from Denmark Street. Just like Liverpool FC, we love setting records! We set another record by being the first wedding to take place in our new church building that was now located in Townsend Street. It had moved from its previous location as part of the redevelopment of Brown Square that caused everyone to move; even the church had to go.

Wedding Day 4th November 1972

Our Wedding Reception was held in the Treetops Hotel on the east side of Belfast where the only disaster of the day was the wedding cake! Kathleen had insisted that the wedding cake be made by a friend of her family, who likewise insisted that we receive it as a wedding gift. We had planned to order the cake from someone else, but Kathleen was too nice a person to cause any offence, so she accepted the offer of the cake as a gift. I have to admit, that on the day it looked great! However, when Kathleen and I stood up to cut the cake, the photographer told us to wait on his cue. When he finally gave us the nod, we proceeded to cut the cake together, but to our horror, the knife would not cut through the icing no matter how much we tried.

One of the hotel staff offered to help, but even they could not cut through what was rock solid icing. We tried to laugh it off, but we were seriously embarrassed, Kathleen even more so than me as she was the one who had put her faith in the person who had made the cake. Eventually, the uncut cake was whisked away by a member of the hotel staff. We thought we could hear the sound of a chainsaw coming from the kitchen, but within ten minutes our Wedding Cake was back and properly sliced portions were being served to our guests with tea and coffee, with no shortage of comments regarding the hardness of the icing. I'll now let Kathleen tell you about the honeymoon!

Kathleen writes: "When the reception was over, we were driven off to our honeymoon. Jackie went all out on a no-expense-spared honeymoon in Portrush, which is on the coast about 60 miles north of Belfast. Our good friends Desi Burgess and Elizabeth Barr drove us to Portrush after the wedding reception and dropped us off at a B&B. Desi was from Carrickfergus, and Elizabeth, who is now his wife, was my very special and life-long friend from Brown Square. She was not only one of my best friends growing up, but she was also my Chief Bridesmaid. We had planned to stay for a week as we'd only ever been to Portrush on day trips or for a weekend with a church group, but a whole week of honeymooning in Portrush was going to be something else! Well at least that was the plan. But it was November, and it was cold on the north coast! In fact, it was so cold we had to ask the woman who owned the B&B for a heater for our room. Jackie was embarrassed to ask for it. After all, we were on our honeymoon! But honeymoon or not, we were still cold.

"Well, Tuesday arrived, and we were only halfway through our one-week honeymoon, but because everything to be seen in Portrush can be seen in one day, and we'd seen it all a few times, we decided to take a walk along the beach. As we did so, we soon noticed that no one else was around: I mean no one, anywhere. The streets were empty and the beach was empty. We were, in fact, the only two people along with a few seagulls that looked colder than us. So, right there and then, while sitting on the beach, we decided to cut our honeymoon short and leave for home. But the most important thing was that our married life had begun, and that I was now Mrs Kathleen McKee, a soldier's wife."

Jackie almost shot me

Kathleen continues: "I remember our first home as Mr & Mrs McKee. It was an upstairs maisonette just off the Ballysillan Road, about three miles north of Denmark Street. We had our little maisonette looking well. Walls papered 70s style, ceilings painted, and rooms all furnished in case we had guests. We loved it there. The only drawback was that whatever way we travelled back and forward between our little maisonette and Denmark Street, or to church and back home, we had to travel through, or travel past the community where Bobby McComb had been tortured and killed. Driving along that way was not a problem in itself, but it could have been if we were stopped and challenged by those patrolling the area as IRA vigilantes, especially with Jackie being in the UDR.

"We didn't have a car when we got married, but we had a motorbike! Well, Jackie had a motorbike. I loved riding on the back of that bike in my leather jacket and helmet, feeling warm and safe with my arms firmly wrapped around Jackie's waist. I remember during the first year of our marriage, the bike had been purposely set on fire outside our maisonette, and so it was off the road for repairs, which meant we had to get the bus to church. On a particular Sunday evening, after church, we called into our parent's homes in Denmark Street, and after having tea and a sandwich, we made our way on foot to the bus stop to catch a bus back to our maisonette. However, in doing so, we had to leave Denmark Street at the point where Jackie used to close the gate and lock us in, but now instead of walking back to Brown Square, we were making our way to the bus stop that happened to be at the start of the Catholic community.

"As we approached the bus stop, I remember we were threatened by three men who had seen us coming out of Denmark Street. They knew we were Protestants, but they did not know Jackie was in the UDR, and they certainly did not know he was carrying a gun. I remember they came at us with bottles in their hands and were chanting, "IRA, IRA" as they chinked the bottles against each other. I was so frightened that I turned to run back to Denmark Street, but Jackie pushed me into a shop doorway and told me to stay there. He then stepped out in front of the three men. I thought he'd pulled the gun on them, but he later told me that all he did was to remove the safety catch and point it in their direction from inside his jacket pocket.

"They seemed to have understood what was happening and immediately began to walk backwards until they came to a wall. They quickly got behind the wall, and within just a few moments one of them came out and ran into one of the nearby streets. I again wanted us to make our way back to Denmark Street, but Jackie said we should wait until the bus came, as it was due anytime. After several minutes, the men who were hiding behind the wall came into the open and started shouting at us. Jackie feared that the one who had run away had come back and that they were now possibly armed or had someone else with them, and so he told me to stay inside the shop doorway.

"I was really frightened, and as I stood there shaking, an army truck filled with soldiers drove by. Jackie waved and called out to them in the hope they would stop, but they just waved back and drove on, thinking it was someone cheering them on! The three men were still shouting at us and were becoming even more threatening, but then the bus finally turned into the Antrim Road. As soon as it came to a halt Jackie took me by the hand and quickly got me onto the bus and sat me down on a seat. With gun in hand, but concealed, he went back and stood at the door of the bus until it passed the men who were still standing in the street. As it did so, we could see one of the three men standing with a gun in his hand and with a look on his face that seemed to suggest he knew that he and his friends had missed an opportunity. I was sitting on the bus thinking, 'If only they knew how lucky they were."

That was a scary night for Kathleen, and also for me if I'm honest! Most women in Northern Ireland were not directly involved in the conflict, although many were connected to someone who was, and many would have been witnesses to the conflict, but often from a distance. Kathleen just happened to marry someone who wore the uniform of a British Soldier, and while she was obviously supportive of the choice I'd made while we were still engaged, yet like many others, she had no idea that she would face some serious stuff that not only could have ended the life of her UDR husband, but hers also.

During the first year of our married life, and just shortly after the incident on the Antrim Road; our Yamaha was back on the road and we had gone to church for our midweek Bible Study. I always left my personal firearm in the drawer of Pastor Billy Mullan's desk, but not before removing the magazine containing the bullets, which I kept in my pocket during the service. At the end of the Bible Study, I picked up the gun as normal, and like Clint Eastwood in a Dirty Harry movie, I would put the gun into a spring-loaded holster under my jacket. Off we then went, climbing onto the Yamaha with Kathleen holding on tight. As we were riding back to our little maisonette, we were going along the Old Park Road. Everything was normal until we were suddenly stopped at a British Army Checkpoint who had used their jeeps to block the road. There was obviously a serious security situation occurring and so the soldiers were not taking time to explain to anyone what was happening. They just directed us into Ardoyne - the area where our friend Bobby McComb had been murdered. We had to go back the way we came or go through Ardoyne. I chose to go through Ardoyne.

I told Kathleen to hold on tight and that I was not stopping for anyone. Kathleen had never at any time been in Ardoyne before that moment, and the thought of taking a tour through its streets was certainly not on her bucket list; it was terrifying. So, here we were riding through Ardoyne, a community of around 9,000 Catholics, but controlled by IRA vigilantes. There were dozens of streets that all looked much the same, with hundreds of homes and fenced off gardens, a place where a stranger could easily get lost. When we got to the end of the first street, there was a group of six men standing at the corner. I spoke to

Kathleen and told her to stay calm, as it was important that we did not look nervous and that we did not give away the fact that we were strangers to the area.

When we got to the end of the street, the men were standing on the right, and so I decided to turn left, although I had no idea where left would take us. But as soon as I made the turn I was horrified, because I had turned into a dead-end street that was blocked off by a barricade. I was concerned that the men at the corner were now awakened to the fact that we were strangers. I shouted to Kathleen to hold on and immediately swung the bike around. In a moment we were speeding in the other direction. Kathleen gripped me so tightly around the waist it was clear she was terrified. Thankfully I found the way out of Ardoyne and soon we were home.

Kathleen picks up the story from here... "As soon as we entered our little maisonette, we felt safe, and so Jackie took his gun from its holster, as he did every time he got home. He continued to make sure the gun was cleared and safe. I thought nothing of it, but went on into the living room and switched on the television. No sooner had I done so and sat down, when Jackie walked into the living room holding the gun in his hand, gesturing that something was wrong. He then told me he had forgotten to put the magazine back into the gun when he retrieved it from the pastor's desk. He then reminded me, as if I'd needed such reminding, that we had just ridden through the middle of Ardoyne with an unloaded gun. I really understood what the implications were, but Jackie continued anyway to explain what he would have done if someone had stopped and challenged us.

"Now anyone who knows him knows he's the kind of person who could not talk without using his hands. For example, Jackie could not talk about Stevie Wonder playing the piano without giving a demonstration with his fingers moving across the ivories. With that in mind, there he was, with gun in hand, explaining to me he would have pointed the gun at anyone who might have approached us (and at this stage, he was actually pointing the gun in my direction). He then said that if he'd needed to, he would have pulled the trigger, which is exactly what he did while talking to me, and bang! The gun went off! A bullet came flying in my direction. It turned out that a bullet had been left in the chamber of the gun that had failed to eject when he left the gun in the pastor's office.

"Fortunately, for both of us, he knew not to point a gun directly at anyone unless he intended to actually shoot them, and I knew he wasn't intending to shoot me as we were only in our first year of marriage. But here we were, and a gun goes off in our living room! It all happened in the blink of an eye. One moment Jackie was standing looking at me and the next moment, bang! Thankfully the bullet missed me and hit the wall right next to me. It put a hole in the wall to my right, hit the ceiling above me, then hit the wall to my left, and finally the bullet landed right at my feet. It all happened in what seemed like just a single moment. I sat there in total shock and just stared at him, and all he did was stare back in total silence, looking every bit as shocked as I was. We seriously did not say a word for what seemed like several minutes, although in all honesty it was probably just seconds. We finally broke the silence with a hug."

It took Kathleen and me a few days to get over what had happened that night, but you can be sure that we were both so thankful that it didn't end as it could have done. That night, death came knocking unexpectedly on Kathleen's door, albeit by accident at the hands of her soldier husband; but death was not God's plan for Kathleen McKee.

The same make of gun that almost took Kathleen's life - 32 Browning.

Chapter 3

Car Bombs versus Bible College

For several days we told no one about the gun going off accidentally and about Kathleen's near-death experience. We simply remained thankful to God that we were both okay. We were still alive, still in love, and still together, but Kathleen not only loved me; she loved Jesus and was deeply committed to serving Him by any means and in any way, and so one of the first things we did as a newly married couple was to open our maisonette for an all-night prayer meeting on the last Friday of each month. Some of our friends and youth leaders came along and joined us. We would drink tea and coffee, read the Bible and discuss what we read, and would then pray for a while. We would repeat this routine a few times through the night as it helped keep us awake and keep us focused. We loved it, and we loved our church. Church became our second home, perhaps even our first.

We lived in the maisonette for one year, but before moving to another home, our beloved Yamaha motorcycle had seen its last days. The fire was too much for it. Someone obviously didn't like us, but we had no idea that God might well have been preparing us for future ministry that would involve much more than the burning of a bike, it wasn't only the fire that saw its demise. Coming off it a few times didn't help, especially one Sunday morning when I offered our Pastor, Billy Mullan, a ride home after the service. His car had been off the road for repairs, so he happily threw his leg over the back of the bike, and with several of our church family looking on and waving as we set off, with my excitement I hit the throttle a bit too much, and so with his weight on the back, the front of the bike went straight upwards towards space and we both tumbled to the ground. Although I was slightly embarrassed, I was okay but my pastor had a limp for several days afterwards! But with the Yamaha now gone we decided to buy our first car, a second-hand light blue Vauxhall Viva.

We had each other, we had our little maisonette, and we now had our first car! Things were still moving forward. We left our maisonette and moved back to Denmark Street into a three-bedroom house, No. 9, right next to both of our parents, but also surrounded by many old friends and neighbours from Brown Square including Bobby McComb's parents, and Sammy and Violet Miller (Bobby's sister). It was like being home, and Kathleen loved it, but it would not be without its challenges, as Kathleen now explains.

"I was so excited when we were given the opportunity to move to our new home in Denmark Street. Not only were we closer to our families and friends, but we were also closer to the church, and having three bedrooms meant we could do so much more for others. Jackie and I had always said we wanted to use our home to serve God and to help people, and so we opened our home and had people stay with us for different reasons, including visitors from the first Elim Church in Dublin, Jackie's uncle Sandy from New Zealand, and one very special young man from East Belfast who was like a young brother to Jackie. His name was Davy Douglas.

"Although Jackie was in the UDR, he started as part-time and when he was not on duty, he worked for a furniture company, where he started as a van driver doing deliveries but was later promoted to Dispatch Manager. One of the young men who worked there with him was Davy Douglas. Davy was 19 years old, but his mother had died when he was in a Young Offenders Centre. Jackie would often bring him back to our home for dinner, when he would sit and tell us about his mother who was a Christian and would tell us about his family in East Belfast.

"He told us that his father, who he lived with, was a member of the UVF, but Davy was in another group called the Young Tartans that became part of the UDA. My heart went out to Davy, and although I was just a few years older than he was, I became like a mother to him. Life was anything but good for Davy, which is why Jackie began to reach out to him, bringing him to our church youth group where Jackie was one of the leaders, and where Davy began to connect with some of the young people in the group. He loved it and felt that this is where his mother would want him to be.

"Davy would stop off at our home on his way to work in the mornings and have breakfast with us. He would never eat eggs as he had a stomach ulcer, and apparently, eggs upset his ulcer, but he ate plenty of toast and anything else that was on the go. Later on, he began to stay overnight. That started on Monday nights after the youth group, which meant he could just travel to work the next morning with Jackie, but this then developed to him staying other nights during the week. He became like family. He was like a young brother to Jackie and like a grown-up son to me.

"But then one day we got the heart-breaking news that Davy had been kidnapped along with another person he'd been working with. It was all over the news. I don't know much about the reason why, but I do know at that time there was a fall-out between the person Davy was with, and the UDA in East Belfast where Davy was from. Sadly, Davy just happened to be in the wrong place at the wrong time, and now he was listed among the disappeared. Jackie and I were heartbroken. We hoped for the best but feared the worst. We felt like we had lost someone in our own family because to us he was family.

"Jackie and I prayed together for Davy every night for several months. We prayed he would be found and that he would still be alive. In fact, there was not a night during those months that we did not kneel beside each other on our living room floor and pray for him. We even had his photo on top of the television to remind us of him and to remind us to pray. However, several months later, the day we had both expected and feared, finally came. Two bodies had been found in a shallow grave, and our worst nightmare was confirmed when it was reported that the bodies found were those of Davy Douglas and the other person he'd been with. We were devastated.

"It really did feel like we had lost a family member, like we'd lost a brother who was just a few years younger than us. But we were so thankful for the times we had spent with Davy, and for the influence I know we both had on his life. I had cooked for him and washed his clothes, and got medicine to help ease the pain of the ulcer he had constantly complained about. Our home in Denmark Street felt empty again, but I had no idea that Davy would not be the last young man who would stay at our home, although not for the same reason."

Davy had such a bond with Kathleen and me. It was like we were his proxy family. He was making so many right choices out of respect for the memory of his late mother, often speaking very fondly of her. I never met his father, although he did speak of him often but always in relation to his father being a member of the Ulster Volunteer Force (UVF). When the details of his death finally came out it was revealed that he and the person he was with had been picked up by members of the UDA and were handed over to members of the UVF who carried out the assassinations.

When death came knocking – again!

Kathleen and I were back home in Denmark Street, but home was not what it used to be. Yes, we were once again surrounded by family and friends; and yes, we still had that old neighbourly spirit that we had enjoyed so much when we were in Brown Square, but there was always something that seemed to be trying to destroy whatever good we had as a tight community, and for some reason also trying to destroy us as a young couple who were devoted to each other and devoted to serving God. That something often came as a spirit of death seeking another unsuspecting victim, a spirit that came too close for comfort on several occasions. Kathleen shares the following story of one of those nights when death came knocking again:

"I loved our home in Denmark Street. I loved being back among family and friends, besides being close to the church. I was also within walking distance of the Ladybird where I worked as a stitcher, but sadly our little section of the street with its twelve houses was to experience more than its fair share of heartache. Not only were we living a few doors from where Bobby McComb had lived with his parents before he was murdered, but as previously stated, we had lost young Davy Douglas. As if that wasn't enough, two others were shot, and an attempt was also made on Jackie's life - all within this little section of Denmark Street.

"One of our neighbours directly opposite our home was also a friend and was one of Jackie's colleagues in the UDR. Michael Riley would travel back and forth with Jackie to their base camp at Girdwood Barracks. They did this three times one week and then four times the following week. This was their routine, but Jackie always knew that any established pattern was dangerous.

"One morning, as part of his normal routine, Jackie was preparing to leave home around 3.30am to go on duty at 4am. He was tiptoeing around the bedroom so as not to awaken me, although that never worked, especially when the alarm would go off at 3am. As Jackie was being as quiet as he could, he heard a sudden noise coming from the street. He gently lifted back the curtains and looked in the direction of his car, and to his horror, he could see two men. One of them was standing alongside his car while the other was lying on his back and was partly underneath it.

"Jackie looked across the street and noticed that Michael was also at his window, looking into the street. He immediately motioned with hand signals (no mobile phones in those days), indicating to Michael to meet him in the street. As he left the room, he told me to stay where I was, and to not even look out of the window. Off he went with gun in hand to meet Michael and confront the two men at the car. I sat up in the bed and just waited. I was terrified, but all I could do was wait, and pray. We had no house phone so I couldn't call anyone. I just prayed that God would protect Jackie and Michael.

"It wasn't long before he was back and told me that as he and Michael were stepping over the walls between the gardens, one of them made a noise and the two men ran off. Jackie reported what had happened to his Commanding Officer and it was soon confirmed that the men had attempted to attach an explosive device underneath his car. The men escaped, but Jackie and Michael also escaped - with their lives. Sadly, Michael would later die at the hands of two gunmen who burst into his Denmark Street home and gunned him down while he was watching a football match on television."

Kathleen and I had no idea that our move to Denmark Street would be a challenging and painful one. There was no doubt that 'The Troubles' were having a huge impact on both of our lives and on the lives of those around us: people like those we have mentioned and others; but it wouldn't end there. Another attempt was made on my life when a gunman fired five shots at me from a distance of 30 feet. Thankfully, he missed with every shot. Yet, regardless of all that had happened during those challenging years, Kathleen and I remained faithful and committed to each other and faithful and focused on our commitment to Christ and our local church where we were both involved in working with young people and children. I worked with young people and Kathleen with children.

Kathleen writes as follows: "If I had a calling on my life, it was working with children. My friend Elizabeth and I were often referred to as the

Pied Pipers of Denmark Street. We would often be seen walking dozens of children through the streets of the Lower Shankill and meeting up with another friend, Jean Johnston, who was likewise walking children through the streets. Together, we walked to the children's meeting at church, called Sunshine Corner. It was aptly named because it really did bring a little bit of sunshine to the lives of those children, and also to ours.

"While my life was focused on working with children, Jackie and I had no children of our own until January 1976, when our first child was born on the 16th of that month. I had always liked the name Jonathan, the name of King David's friend, who was faithful to David even in some very difficult situations. And so, I wanted to call our firstborn son Jonathan, believing he would be faithful in all circumstances. I had no idea that one day he would join and stand faithfully alongside Jackie as a pastor in the church. So, he was rightly named, but we also called him David as a middle name, not after King David, but in memory of Davy Douglas who had been murdered.

"We were excited that we were now parents and that we were on that part of our journey where we had started our own family; excited that another child was born not just into the McKee and the McDermott family, but into the Denmark Street community. Jackie was now a dad and a very proud one at that. Everything was looking good, except for the sleepless nights that came along with having a baby, and there were many. However, when Jonathan was only six months old, tragedy struck on my side of the family as death came knocking once again; only this time it was at the door of my older brother, Geordie McDermott.

"We had been attending our church barbecue when we received news that Geordie had been shot several times and was very seriously ill in hospital. He had been shot while driving his Shankill Taxi. Two men had gotten into the taxi on the Crumlin Road, but unknown to Geordie, the men were in the IRA and were armed. No sooner had Geordie set off with the two men in the back seat, when one of them called out, telling him to pull over at the next stop. This was strange because they'd only just got in. Geordie immediately became suspicious but had no idea what would happen next. As soon as he pulled over and stopped, the men got out, and as they did so, one of them produced a gun. The passenger, sitting next to Geordie in the front of the taxi, was shot in the head and killed instantly. Geordie was shot seven times, but amazingly, and thankfully, he survived.

"Geordie had six bullets removed from his body. Both of his lungs had been punctured, and he was so badly injured that the surgeon told us all that we should expect the worst. They were fully expecting him to die, but thank God for the expertise of the surgeon, excellent nursing staff, and lots of prayer. This included my own father, who prayed on his knees for Geordie every night, even though he wasn't himself a Christian at that time. But with all those prayers and with all that help, Geordie pulled through within a couple of weeks and has been doing well for over 40 years, even though he still carries a bullet in his body."

Hearing from God on the stairs

It's quite obvious from Kathleen's comments that the first few years of our married life were anything but uneventful. The 1970s were difficult years for many reasons. We had started our own family in the 70s and, regardless of all that was going on around us, we thought we were settled in our new home that we had worked hard at and had it looking so well. Kathleen continued to work with the children at the church and within our local community in Denmark Street and around the Lower Shankill, but she also loved to connect with the women in the church, which she did faithfully every Wednesday night at the mid-week Women's Meeting. This meant me staying at home baby-sitting Jonathan on what were normally quite uneventful Wednesday nights. But I'll let Kathleen explain what happened on one of those nights.

Kathleen writes, "Every Wednesday night I would go to the women's meeting at church. We would sing a few choruses and someone would share a brief Bible study or a testimony. We would then have a wee cup of tea and a piece of cake or something before going home. I remember coming home from one of those meetings. It was February 1977. Jonathan had only just had his first birthday a few weeks earlier on 16th January. While I was out at the women's meeting, Jackie was babysitting. When I got home that night, Jackie looked tearful, like he'd been crying. I asked what was wrong and he explained that when he had put Jonathan to bed that night, he was coming back down the stairs when he believed God spoke to him about going to Bible College.

"Jackie had mentioned Bible College before, but it was never as serious as this. In fact, the way he was talking, he sounded and looked like he was ready, right there and then, for Bible College. I half expected him to tell me that his bags were packed and that he'd be leaving for college. My immediate thoughts were of our home and of everything we had worked so hard for and of the family we were planning to have and the family we already had, and I thought of our friends and of church. I felt a real sense of uncertainty, and so my first reaction was not what it probably should have been, because I was the one who was now tearful and to be perfectly honest, they were not tears of joy.

"But then the same God who spoke to Jackie that Wednesday night also spoke to my heart not long after. I remember one night while lying in bed that I just began to cry. Jackie asked me what was wrong, and I said to him, "It's Bible College. I believe God is saying we should go." I then told him he should go ahead and apply, saying that we needed to do this together. Within a few days, Jackie spoke to our pastor, Billy Mullan, and even though Pastor Mullan was excited for us and encouraged us to keep praying into this, he advised that we should apply for the following year, but we both felt it was right to strike while the iron in our hearts was still hot. So, Jackie applied to attend the Elim Bible College in England in 1977.

"My role was to go along with him for the next two years and support him however possible. One of the ways I did so was to work in the college to help pay for tuition fees and to pay for our food and accommodation as a family. But while my working in the college was to help, we knew we still needed more, and so we made some major changes and personal sacrifices, like giving up our home and everything in it. We'd been living in our Denmark Street home for four years, and although we didn't own it, we did own everything in it in terms of fixtures and furniture, except the television, which we rented from a shop on the Shankill Road where we'd call in once a week to pay the rent.

"To be honest, I admit that leaving our home was much harder for me than it was for Jackie, but we did so together. We sold every piece of furniture we owned so we could pay for college fees and expenses, but what we raised by selling the furniture was only enough to cover the first of two years at college. My older brother Geordie and his wife Sis (Sarah) and family, were able to move into our home as the new tenants of No. 9 Denmark Street. What helped us even more was that they bought some of our furniture and appliances.

"I was so delighted it was my brother and his wife who were the ones moving into what had been our home for four years. They moved in several months before we went to Bible College, and so we moved in with my mum and dad who lived just across the street. We stayed with them rent-free for the next few months, giving us a chance to save for college. We were making lots of sacrifices, but the biggest sacrifice for Jackie was having to eat my mum's stew every Wednesday for dinner; not that he didn't like stew; he just didn't like my mum's stew. Before we would ever be served, he would be screwing up his face when mum was not looking, swallowing it without trying to taste it, and the reason why? Mum put turnip into it, plenty of it also!"

As Kathleen shows, going to Bible College was not the easiest thing in the world to do. Going somewhere new was one thing, but leaving where we'd been settled was something else! The last thing to be sold was our Vauxhall Viva. We held on to that for as long as we could, but then came the day when we had to let it go, which for the first time in our married life left us without any kind of transport.

However, we had made friends with two very special people, Paul and Annette Stevens. They were from Apsley Street Elim Church in South Belfast, and they were also going to the Elim Bible College in England at the same time as us.

Paul and Annette were a Godsend, not just for their friendship, but more so for the fact that they still owned a car and that they were driving to Bible College. They also had a little girl who was the same age as Jonathan, and so for the first year, we were able to hitch a ride backwards and forwards with them. Kathleen and I deeply appreciated their practical support, but more to the point is that we remain thankful for the lifelong friendship that was established between us.

Chapter 4

The Week Elvis Died

At the end of August 1977, about a week after Elvis tragically died, we were leaving Kathleen's parents' home. We left Belfast on a ferry to Scotland. As the ferry pulled away, we made our way to the stern; that's the Navy Cadet training coming out! We stood there for a while, looking back at Belfast, knowing this would be our longest time ever away from home and family. We were already beginning to feel homesick, but we knew in our hearts that we were in the right place and on the right path.

When we docked in Scotland, we headed off into the night in Paul and Annette's car. Kathleen and I were in the back seat, while Jonathan and Leslie-Anne were laid out on blankets behind the back seats where they would sleep for the entire length of the journey. From Scotland, we drove south into England along the M6, stopping off at service stations for teas and coffees until we finally arrived at college early the next morning. This became a return journey we would make with Paul and Annette three times during our first year, but if the truth were told, the driving backwards and forwards was the easiest part of our entire journey. Kathleen explains why:

"The journey from Belfast across to Scotland and down through England to Bible College was long and tiresome, but, as Jackie said, that was the easy part. This was a journey that involved more than driving down the M6 in England. It was a journey that began with giving up our home and selling everything we had worked and saved for, everything except our clothes and a few blankets and some of Jonathan's toys. I can tell you as a wife and a mother, that that was one of the most difficult things I ever had to do, and yet it was not the hardest. No! Leaving our families and friends back home in Belfast, and not being able to go out shopping with my sisters Marie and Sally on Saturdays, was the hardest thing. We had taken Jonathan away from his four grandparents. We had also left our extended family and our church family which was the only spiritual home we had known, and had gone to a very different place, a place called Bible College.

"When we first arrived and signed in, we were taken to our accommodation that would be our home for at least the first year. I remember that day walking into our room. It was a small room with a double bed and a single bed, two wardrobes, a desk and a chair. I remember lying on the bed that first night and looking around our tiny room and crying. I wanted to go back to Denmark Street. I could not hold back how I was feeling, and so I told Jackie that night that I wanted to go home, and to my surprise, he agreed with me! He was feeling exactly as I was. He told me he would arrange for us to return, but it was late, we were tired and needed to sleep. When morning came, we talked more about what was happening, and even though we shared how we were feeling, we agreed we would stay at the college until the Christmas break and then go home and not return. Well, that was our plan...

"However, when Christmas came and we were back in Belfast staying at my parent's home, we talked again about college and agreed we would go back until Easter. I think it was my mum's stew that did it! (Joking of course) But that's how we went through our time at Bible College, by saying we would return home at the end of each term and that we'd not return, but we always did. We both agreed that my mum's stew was good preparation for Bible College food. You see, God always knows what He's doing - even stew made with turnip has a purpose!

"Our little single room during our first year was in the college annexe and was next door to the head of catering. She was called Miss White, and was the kind of person you needed to make sure was on your side, or at least you made sure you were never on her wrong side! Having said that, I managed to get on well with her. At times I would sit with her while Jackie was at lessons. Sometimes Jonathan would wander into her little room on his own. One day he came back into our room with a hard sweet in his hand that Miss White had given him. We watched as he put the sweet into his mouth, and in a moment, it stuck in his throat. His little face went from red to purple in moments. He looked at us with such a helpless look on his face as he couldn't breathe.

"I cried out while Jackie grabbed him and began to shake him and slap him on the back, but the sweet was firmly lodged in his throat and he wasn't breathing. Knowing that time was not on our side, Jackie then did what we're always told not to do with someone who's choking. He put his finger into the back of Jonathan's throat and was able to pull the sweet right out. The whole thing must have taken all of one minute, but it was a long minute filled with fear because it really did look like we were losing him. But the fear quickly turned to joy and relief when I could see that Jackie's reaction had saved Jonathan's life. However, my nerves were still getting the better of me, and as soon as we had settled down, I went directly into Miss White's room to let her know what had happened. I was still shaking, and I have to admit I was really angry. You can be sure that Miss White never did give Jonathan anymore hard sweets after that."

As Kathleen and I have spent time chatting and looking back, even at moments like Jonathan almost choking on a sweet, I can't help but think that the fact we made it through our first year, and that we were still at Bible College, was a miracle in itself. There is no doubt that God had His hand on us as a family and had provided for us in so many ways. For example, every time we went home from college, some of the people in our home church would hand us an envelope with cash inside, and then on other occasions we would receive a card or letter in the mail that contained cash or a cheque, and it was this that got us through each term and enabled us to pay our share of the travel costs to get us back and forth from home to college.

Paying our way through Bible College with the support of others was one thing; living as a family and trying to maintain family life was still a necessity that I never lost sight of. It helped when we returned home at the end of each term to be able to preach in some churches. But hey, this is Northern Ireland, and while that gave some much-needed experience, it didn't really help put food on the table, especially when I was sent packing from one church for reading from the Revised Standard Version of the Bible rather than from the version used by Peter and Paul, i.e. The King James Version! (smile)

I took on some part-time work wherever I could get it, including driving a black taxi on the Shankill Road for Kathleen's brother Geordie (the one who'd been shot), besides working as a labourer in Redland Tiles. This was thanks to the late Alfie McCrory senior, who was able to 'put a word in for me'. The hardest thing about working in Redland Tiles was not that I had to catch newly-made roof tiles before they fell off the end of a conveyer belt while being outside during winter, but having to leave the house at 6am, as the factory was outside Belfast. However, not wanting to be outdone, but also wanting to do her bit to put something on the table, Kathleen took on part-time work in two shops; one a shoe shop and the other a shop selling goods for the home; but Kathleen will share her experience as a postwoman.

"I didn't mind working in the shops. In fact, I quite enjoyed doing so as I enjoyed meeting people and chatting. But there was one job I really hated, and that was being a postwoman during the Christmas break. It paid good money, but it was so difficult getting out of bed and out of the house by 5am each morning. Doing some late-night shifts didn't help either. I found it tough being a postwoman, but I knew I had to stick with it, like the stamps on the corners of the envelopes I was carrying. So stick with it I did. But then, to be honest, I needed Jackie's help. I needed him to help me with the post, and so he would come out with me and would drive along the street with the full bag of cards inside the car that I'd been given to deliver. This made it so much easier because it meant I just needed to carry a handful of cards at a time, rather than the whole bag. But between the two of us, we got the job done and we got the Christmas mail delivered on time.

"We were doing life together, so a few part-time jobs and being a postwoman over Christmas, along with the support of friends and family, helped us make it through. So, when our first year was coming to an end, it was clear even to me that our lives had changed and would probably never be the same. I was a mother and a wife, but I no longer had a home. My home in Denmark Street was well and truly gone: the home where Jonathan had spent his first year; the home where we had entertained guests from the new Elim Church in Dublin; the home that had become Davy Douglas's second home before he was murdered was now gone. I had survived the first year in a single room at Bible College; a year of working in the college, cleaning out lecture rooms and offices, besides doing a bit of gardening, so that I was either pushing a vacuum cleaner or pushing a wheelbarrow, and doing so as Jackie studied. I have to admit, it was tough, but what kept me going was that I knew that although I had not married a pastor, I was helping to make one."

First year at College ends in tragedy

It was during our final few weeks in June, that someone came knocking on our room door to let me know there was a phone call for me over in the main college. They said it was urgent, and so I ran across to the only phone used by students. It was my mum. She was crying. Through the sobs, she managed to tell me that Michael Riley had been shot and that it wasn't thought he would make it. I remember walking back to my room with tears streaming down my face and with feelings of anger I had not felt for some time. When I shared the news with Kathleen, we both sat and cried. There was nothing else we could do other than pray for him and his wife who was also called Kathleen. Michael hung on for two months, but he finally passed away during August, and while we'd be home for his funeral, even more tragedy was to strike before our first year at college came to an end and before we returned to Belfast.

Kathleen and I had joined the College Choir, led by Evangeline Vandenburg, wife of Peter Vandenburg who since leaving Bible College has worked for many years with Reinhard Bonnke and with Daniel Kolenda at Christ for all Nations. The choir presented a great opportunity to get connected and to establish new relationships and friendships. One of those we developed a great relationship with was Joy Bath. Joy was one of our Elim missionaries in Zimbabwe, which back then was called Rhodesia. Joy had returned to England to attend the Elim Bible College before returning to join her friends back in Rhodesia, but she never did get back.

Jack, Kathleen on the right with Paul, Annette and Lesley-Anne at the back

On Graduation Day, in June 1978, Kathleen and I, along with the entire college, awakened to the horrific news that all of our Elim missionaries in Rhodesia had been massacred. The only reason Joy survived was the fact that she was with us at Bible College. We had gone through the first year of college in the same class. We had travelled around Elim Churches across the UK together, not just on the occasional choir outing, but most weekends on a ministry team that I had been given the responsibility to lead. Joy and I would sing together as a duet, while sometimes she would sing solo as I accompanied her on guitar.

It was truly devastating and heart-breaking for Joy to hear that all her missionary friends and their children had been murdered. The fact that it happened while she was doing a refresher course in Bible College seemed to add to her pain. All we could do, like many others at the college who knew and loved Joy, was to embrace her and to weep with her. However, Joy was not the only one who was not back in Rhodesia at the time of the massacre. The team leader, Peter Griffiths, was also back in England along with his family at that same time. In fact, Peter Griffiths was booked as our guest speaker at the college graduation that very day, the day we all heard of the massacre, the morning after it had occurred.

Kathleen shares her memories of that morning as follows: "I remember getting Jonathan out of bed to get him washed and dressed so we could go for breakfast. Jackie switched on our black and white television. I can't remember if it was a news programme that was on or if it was a news flash put out for everyone to see, but there on television was a map showing Rhodesia and the news reporter talking about the deaths of British missionaries. Then we heard the Elim Church being mentioned, and so we knew right away they were talking about our missionaries. Jackie and I were stunned. We thought immediately of Joy and wondered what this would do to her. We quickly made our way to the dining hall for breakfast, although breakfast was the last thing on our minds that morning.

"When we got to the dining hall, it seemed like everyone had the same idea. There was an absence of the normal sounds of knives and forks hitting plates and an absence of the noise of general chatter. These had all been replaced with a strange silence. I cannot explain the emotion that filled the dining room and the college that day, as everyone was deeply affected by the news of the massacre. Thirteen of our Elim family had been brutally killed. I remember seeing the principal of the college, Mr Gilpin, speaking with Jackie. He had asked him to meet Peter Griffiths when he arrived at the college car park and to bring him to the principal's office with clear instructions not to mention what had happened in Rhodesia. It was thought that Peter Griffiths did not know of the massacre, and it turned out that he didn't until Mr Gilpin broke the news to him in the office."

Wesley Gilpin had the unenviable task of breaking the worst possible news to Peter Griffiths. The college staff felt it was right to continue with the graduation ceremony, and more importantly, Peter Griffiths, although totally broken, also decided that he would still speak. Everyone would have understood if Peter decided not to speak that day, but he stood in front of a packed marquee. Despite the devastating news he had received, he presented a very moving message that included an illustration of the five American missionaries who had been murdered by the Aucas in Ecuador in January 1956.

This was certainly not how we thought our first year at Bible College would end. We were expecting to go out in a blaze of celebration, like, *"You shall go out with joy and be led forth in peace"* (Isaiah 55:12), but instead, our hearts were heavy; although we knew that those who died had not lived their lives in vain, and neither had they died in vain. So, our first year at Bible College was tough. We went and we came, often saying we'd not go back, but we did; until finally we made it, at least to the end of the first year. However, the way that year ended was unexpected and tragic considering the deaths of the missionaries.

Having completed our first year at college, we were more than ready for our summer break. We had already made plans to spend the first two weeks in France, before returning to Belfast. Kathleen picks it up from here:

"I had only ever been to the mainland of Europe once before Bible College. It was when I was at the Girls Model School and we went on a school trip to Switzerland. I loved it and had always wanted to go back; if not to Switzerland, well, back to somewhere else in Europe. Being at Bible College gave us the ideal opportunity as we were not far from Dover where the ferry departed for Calais in France. So, before returning to Belfast at the end of our first year at college, we decided to take a break in France. At the end of June 1978, we were joined by Desi and Elizabeth, our two friends who had driven us to Portrush for our honeymoon back in 1972, although I should say there was much more to our friendship than just the drive to Portrush.

"Elizabeth and I had been great friends since our childhood days in Brown Square. We lived in the same street, went to the same school, the same church, we had the same interest in working with children, and we both loved singing. Jackie and Desi both played the guitar, and so Elizabeth and Desi, Jackie and me, and another friend called Linda Armstrong, who later became Linda Annette when she married Jim Annette, formed a singing group called Challenge. For several years we sang together in churches across Belfast and Northern Ireland, but that all came to an end when Jackie and I went to Bible College.

"So, it was Desi and Elizabeth who met up with us at Bible College. They stayed for a couple of days, and from there we drove to Dover where we got the ferry across to France. Jackie's sister Kathleen and her husband Len, who was a continental fitter for Mackie's Engineering Factory in Belfast, lived in France at that time. This was handy for us because it meant we were able to drive to Kathleen and Len's home and spend a night with them before exploring France. What happened next wasn't funny at the time, but we did laugh afterwards. We had borrowed Len's trailer-tent that we were able to attach to a towbar on the back of the car. Desi was driving, but at one point he took a wrong turn, and without even thinking, he put the car into reverse. As he backed up, we heard a crunch. It was the trailer! It had turned in on itself as Desi was reversing; in a moment, there was a large hole in the side of the trailer-tent. There was nothing we could do and so we kept on driving, deciding to let Len know what happened when we got back.

"Things were going okay. The weather was good, the campsites were good and the food was okay. We were hoping to make it to Paris, but sadly that was not to happen. We'd been in France for less than a week when we got a phone call from home. My sister Sally's 17-year-old son, Robert Sewell, had been killed in a motorbike accident. Jackie and I had talked with him often and would listen to some of his LP records, especially his favourite, Tubular Bells, by Mike Oldfield. Young Robert had been hit by a taxi and was rushed to hospital, but sadly he passed away on 4th July. I couldn't believe it. I sat in the car and cried when Jackie told me what had happened. My heart was broken for my sister Sally. That was the end of our holiday in France. We immediately made our way back to Belfast. Desi and Elizabeth dropped us off at the airport where we got a flight home, while they made their way home by car.

"It was a horrible homecoming! There was no comfort to be given to Sally and her husband Robert, or their two daughters, Anne and Valerie. In fact, even after all these years, I know it's something that Sally has never got over. She relives the pain of Robert's loss often, and especially every 4th July."

Our second year at college

It would be an understatement to say that the summer of 1978 was not such a good summer! It began with a phone call letting us know that Michael had been shot. This was soon followed by the news that our missionaries and their families in Rhodesia had been massacred, and then we received the tragic news of the sudden death of our young nephew Robert. Before we returned to Bible College, Michael Riley finally passed away during the month of August. So, no! The summer of '78 was not good.

Besides dealing with the issues we were facing, we were fighting again against the urge to not return to college. We talked and we prayed, and we finally agreed that we should do our best to stay focused on what we had to do and that we would return to Bible College at the end of August. We visited several churches where I'd been booked to speak, as arranged by our then pastor, John Harris. We also managed to do some part-time work wherever we could. However, we did get some time to relax and to plan for our return to Bible College to commence our second year, but to be perfectly honest, we were not really looking forward to it. However, we knew in our hearts that this was something we needed to do and needed to complete. So, at the end of August 1978, we headed back to the Elim Bible College.

The second year was not a walk in the park, but I have to say that it was easier than the first. For a start, we had bought a second-hand car in Belfast for a few pounds with the intention of using it to get us back and forth to college and then disposing of it at the end of our second year. We would drive behind Paul and Annette, following them through Scotland and down the M6 through several English counties to Bible College, but even that wasn't as straightforward as we would have liked! Kathleen explains why:

"I remember one night our car broke down on the M6 in England, and yes it was raining! Why is it always raining when your car breaks down? Anyway, the car we had paid a few pounds for just stopped on the motorway. Paul and Jackie took a look at the engine and saw that the fan belt had snapped. He then went through our bags until he found a pair of my tights that he proceeded to wrap around some part of the engine where the fan belt once was, and lo and behold, it worked. The engine started and off we went. My tights got us to our destination. They were probably the best part of the car, which to be honest wasn't up to much, but it helped to make things so much easier during our second year at Bible College.

"Another thing that helped during our second year was that we were able to move from our single room to another part of the college where we had our own little self-catering flat. It meant we were not having to pay for college food, which was a blessing for two reasons; we were saving on our overall expenses, and we no longer had to eat college soup with leftover eggs mixed in! It was above one of the lecturer's homes, Christopher Gornold-Smith and his wife Ragna. They were two amazing people who let Jackie use their storeroom as his secret study and prayer place, and who reached out to us in a friendly way to help make our stay more comfortable. Ragna invited me several times into her home for tea and a chat. In fact, the first time she brought me in she made me coffee. I didn't have the heart to tell her I didn't drink coffee, so I just sipped away at it as best I could.

"From here on and throughout the year, and with college food now behind us, it was beans and toast all the way, but that was okay because what mattered was that we were making it in our own little kitchen and were serving it on our own little dining table! It was almost like home, only without my mum's stew! Another reason that the year was easier, was that Jonathan now had his own bedroom, which meant I could watch my black and white TV while Jackie was studying, without keeping Jonathan awake. Our bedroom was part of the living room, but it was still a far cry from the tiny little room we'd all shared back in the main college.

"So, things were much better but it was still tough. We still had our struggles, but we were so thankful for these blessings as they helped make the second year so much better and helped us get through to Jackie's graduation in June 1979, and to us eventually completing our time at college, something we had often doubted would happen. Our time at college was now finally over and we were heading back to Northern Ireland where I'd once again have a normal home to look after. At least that's what I thought, but more of that later."

Moving beyond college

It would be another understatement to say that Kathleen was glad our time at Bible College was over and equally glad that we were on our way back home. While it was easy enough for both of us to leave college behind, there was at least one thing that was not so easy, and that was the fact that we were departing from friends that we had got to know and love during those two years. It was like we were all in it together regardless of the term years we were in, but now it was over, and we were all going our separate ways, leaving many friends who we would never meet again. While a few of us got back to Northern Ireland, others were dispersed throughout Scotland, Wales, England, and further afield including South America, Africa, South Africa, India, Sri Lanka, Malaysia and Hong Kong. One of those we said farewell to was Joy Bath, mentioned earlier. Joy was not able at that time to return to Rhodesia/Zimbabwe, because of what had happened to her friends.

However, Joy did return to the mission field. This was her heart and her calling. International Missions was what she lived for. So, after college, she went to India with her friend Olive Jarvis, but then later she was able to return to Zimbabwe for a while. None of us can even begin to imagine how Joy must have felt when she returned to the place that held so many memories for her. At times, in her imagination, she must have heard the voices of her friends and the laughter of children playing, with perhaps so many questions and very few answers.

But then the unthinkable happened. While treating someone who had AIDS, Joy was accidentally infected with the AIDS virus. She soon became severely ill and was returned to England where she spent time in hospital in Southampton. She was visited by our friend Paul Stevens, with whom we'd travelled back and forth to college, who at the time of Joy's illness was involved with Elim's International Missions. Sadly, there was nothing the hospital could do to save Joy, and she finally returned to live out her last days with her parents in Salisbury. Kathleen now shares what happened next:

"I remember singing with Joy in the college choir and at times travelling with her and other students to several church services. Joy was such a lovely and gentle person. The thought of her being so ill touched many hearts, especially those who knew her. When Jackie and I heard that Joy was close to passing away, we decided to travel from Belfast to spend some time with her in her home in Salisbury, England. Joy and her parents were delighted to see us. We stayed for several hours, drinking tea, eating sandwiches, and chatting, even laughing as we reminisced about our time together at college and about the times we travelled together and sang together in the college choir. But our hearts were broken as we saw first-hand how AIDS was destroying such a beautiful person. She was much too young and too beautiful to be taken from us in such a manner, but the prayers and the love of many were not able to keep her here, and there was no shortage of either. Before we left their home, Jackie prayed with Joy and her parents, and I remember hugging and kissing Joy on the cheek as we were leaving, and doing so with a sense of heaviness because we knew that unless God miraculously healed her, we would not be seeing Joy again this side of eternity.

"Within just a few days of us returning to Belfast from Joy's home in Salisbury, we received the news that Joy had passed away. It felt like she had gone to join her missionary friends in Heaven who had lost their lives in Rhodesia. Although there was great sadness in her passing, it really did feel like it was meant to be. However, the story didn't end there, because not long after Joy passed away, Peter Griffiths also passed away with cancer. Once again it left us feeling quite strange, knowing they had both missed out on the massacre because they were both in England when it happened, but no matter how much we would try to work it out and to understand why things like this happen, we were left with the thought that only God knows, and that, even from this, some good will come."

And so, Kathleen and I had said farewell to people we had got to know and love while at college, including Joy. Some we would never see again, while others we would see from time to time, if only at the Annual Conference, but it was now time to focus on the future; on our future.

While I had studied Systematic Theology, Old and New Testament Survey, Greek and so much more, Kathleen worked her way through college to help pay the bills along with whatever support we received from our church family and friends back home, and we had made it all the way through to the end, doing so without being in debt to anyone, which in itself was miraculous! Even more miraculous was the fact that at the end of the two years, we had more money in the bank than what we had started with when we left Denmark Street. We had sold all our furniture but were now able to completely furnish our first home in Rathfriland after leaving Bible College, with everything paid for in cash. By the way, if you're asking, "Rathfriland?", so were we! And if you don't know where that is, neither did we! In fact, I had to get a map of Northern Ireland and spread it out on the floor to find out where it was! In the next chapter, Kathleen explains her personal journey that took her from Denmark Street to Rathfriland; from the inner city of Belfast surrounded by concrete structures, buses, and taxis, to a rural community surrounded by fields, cows and sheep.

Chapter 5

My First Challenge as a Pastor's Wife

Kathleen writes: "I'm not sure if any woman ever truly feels called to be a pastor's wife, because I can honestly say that I never did! Well, at least initially, and for some time, I never felt such a call. Yes, I was very much aware of it being something that was on Jackie's heart, but not so much on mine. My attitude was that if Jackie is a soldier, then I'd be a soldier's wife, and I'd be the best soldier's wife possible. If he became a postman, then I'd be a postman's wife, and a good one at that, and I'd maybe even drive the car alongside him with the bag of mail inside while he walked the street delivering the mail. Well, he never did become a postman, although sometimes I know he wishes he had. But he did go from being a soldier to being a pastor, and it was for that reason that I became a pastor's wife, even though I had no idea what that would ultimately mean. Nevertheless, I was still determined to be the best.

"When we left Bible College at the end of June 1979 and returned to Belfast for a few weeks, we stayed again with my parents, before moving on to pastor our first church in Rathfriland and Moneyslane. Jonathan by this time, was 3 years and 6 months, but I was also expecting our second child, and I must admit, I was glad to be home. While Jackie would continue to study, I was finished with cleaning out college rooms and offices and doing work around the college grounds, pushing a wheelbarrow and weeding out rose-beds. My focus was now on being a mother and on being a wife and I was determined to make a success of each of these.

"On the 20th August 1979, I gave birth to our second child, our first daughter. We named her Chara, pronounced *Cara*, which is Greek for Joy. Jackie had studied Greek in our second year at college, and while he did quite well at it, I think this was the only thing he ever took from all those studies. A few weeks later, at the start of September 1979, Jackie was inducted as pastor of the two Elim Churches in Rathfriland and Moneyslane, that were six miles apart.

"The induction service went really well. The Rathfriland church hall was filled with people from both churches, but there were also those who had travelled from Belfast to support us, including members from both our families and friends from our home church. However, it was no great surprise that some of our friends from Belfast ended up in Drogheda, which was across the border in the Republic of Ireland. My friend Margaret McCurley, her husband Billy, and Mabel McKernan, missed the turn to Rathfriland, which shows how well known, or better still how little known Rathfriland was to people living in Belfast. At least they made it to the church in time for supper at the end of the induction service!

"Well, that was it. It was official. Jackie was now formerly a pastor in charge of his first church, and I was now formerly a pastor's wife in charge of tea and sandwiches. It was a great night, and yet unknown to either of us, the first of many challenges was just a matter of hours away: in fact, it was the following morning, before our first church service.

"I had got Jonathan ready in his new Sunday clothes and had got our new baby Chara ready, but then just before we went out through the door, Jackie sat down on a chair in our living room. He looked at me and said, "I'm not doing this! I'm not going through with it." I was stunned. I was shocked, because I was now married to a pastor who didn't want to go to church!

"I remember getting down on one knee and taking Jackie by the hand and telling him it would be okay, that the people would be waiting for him and would be excited to see him, and that he just needed to do this once and everything would be fine. This was my first challenge, to encourage the pastor to actually go to church! I knew that it was such an important moment, and thankfully it worked. Jackie finally stood up and after an encouraging hug, we made our way out of the door and on our way to church. However, I had no idea that greater challenges lay ahead (beyond Rathfriland and Moneyslane); challenges involving power struggles and spiritual attacks from within the church, and then to top that, physical attacks, and death threats from within the community.

"Since that day to this, I've often wondered what life would have been like if I had not talked Jackie out of that chair, and if he had not walked out of that door; but I knew we had not gone through two years of soup with fried eggs, beans and toast, and of carrying out car repairs with a pair of my tights, for it all to end before it really started!

"That morning, we made it to church in plenty of time, and no one was any the wiser as we were warmly greeted by many welcoming and friendly people. I took my seat with Jonathan sitting alongside and with Chara on my knee while Jackie took his place at the front alongside the church elders. The church was full: not just with people, but also with a sense of new expectation. When the time came, Jackie stepped up to the platform, and for the first time ever as a pastor, he welcomed everyone to the service and then proceeded to lead the first hymn, after which he prayed the opening prayer. He then invited everyone to be seated as he shared a few announcements and then led a second hymn. He was doing what he had been taught to do at college, and doing what most other pastors would have done at that time; leading a hymn, saying a prayer, sharing the announcements, and leading another hymn. Everything was going according to plan. I felt so proud of Jackie because he was doing so well, until the end of the second hymn!

"You see at that point; the congregation would normally go into what we called 'a time of open worship' where the service would be left open for people to express thanks to God rather than simply pray prayers. Well, it's how we had experienced church in the past, and it's what we thought happened in every Elim Church. So, when we had finished singing the second hymn, Jackie invited everyone to be seated, and then in his newly acquired pastor's voice, he said, "Can I now invite us all to join together in a time of open worship," Now that was fine in itself, but we were not ready for what happened next, because when Jackie invited the congregation to go into a time of open worship, people around me and across the church stood up. They then turned around and got on their knees. I had no idea what was happening. I looked up and saw a look of bewilderment on Jackie's face as he was still standing on the platform. He likewise had no idea what was happening, but we quickly grasped hold of the fact that this was how they did things in Rathfriland, and so we just went with the flow, and were soon on our knees like everyone else.

"After around 20 minutes on our knees, Jackie invited us all to be seated, he then went back to the platform and preached his first ever sermon as the pastor of a church. The title of that first sermon was, 'Knowing Jesus in the Storm,' and goodness me, didn't we as a couple need to know that Jesus was with us, not only for our first service but in storms we had not even begun to imagine; storms we had not been prepared for during the training at Bible College; storms that would come later.

"The first Sunday morning ended well, but we had two more services that evening, one in Moneyslane at 6 pm and the other back in Rathfriland at 7.30 pm. For the next two and half years it was much the same from one week to the next, being at one church on a Sunday morning, and then being at the other church the following Sunday morning, but then doing two services each Sunday evening, one in each church. During the next two and half years, things remained much the same with the church in Moneyslane, while the church in Rathfriland grew in numbers. Possibly one of the biggest changes the church in Rathfriland had seen was within the first few weeks, when Jackie, with great sensitivity, brought an end to people kneeling during the Sunday morning service, which was something that most people welcomed.

"We did our best to throw everything we had into developing both churches. Jackie would do what was expected of him as the pastor, which was mainly preaching, teaching, and visiting, but it soon became clear that there were additional expectations on me as the pastor's wife. I was immediately thrust into the role of being women's leader and was often brought into discussions with the elder's wives regarding church-related issues. I was not happy with that, but it's what they did. It was a real challenge, as I had never seen myself as a leader, although I did my best to rise to the challenge. We had women's meetings weekly, besides running an annual women's rally with guest speakers and singers, when women from other parts of Northern Ireland would join us.

Sunday laws…

"I learnt a lot from Bible College, from Jackie and more so my own study of the Bible. One thing I was always aware of was that we in the West would often make up laws from our own interpretation of scriptures. For example, some would believe it is not right to watch TV on a Sunday, while for others it did not matter.

"Jackie would often relax on Sunday afternoons after church to watch snooker on TV. Maybe I shouldn't be sharing this, but it's how it was. He loved snooker and there was a Belfast snooker hero called Alex Higgins and there was Steve Davis from England, and there was no missing the snooker final.

"One Sunday afternoon we were watching snooker when someone came to our front door. It was one of our church elders who was visiting unannounced. Jackie immediately went into a panic mode, turning the TV off, grabbing the Elim Church magazine that was sitting on the coffee table and laying it out on the table as if he had been reading it. All I can say is… It's as well he wasn't smoking, or he would have struggled to open the windows! Although, to be clear; he didn't smoke!

"In all honesty, and this might shock a lot of people, but the pretence in some way reflected how we got through those initial ministry years; pretending we were happy when in reality we hated living there. I hope that's not too strong, but it's honest. Pretending everything was okay when everything was far from okay. But to be clear, this is no reflection on the people. We loved the people in Rathfriland and Moneyslane, and they loved us. They looked after us extremely well so that I don't think we ever wanted for anything.

"We never had to buy potatoes the whole time we were there, or carrots or cabbages. It seemed like every time Jackie went to visit someone, he came home with a bag of potatoes and other types of vegetables. In fact, I remember visiting with him at times, and instead of having a cup of tea and a piece of cake handed to us, we were often sat down at the farmhouse table and given a plate of mashed potatoes with butter melted on the top! The people did their best to make us feel at home, but we were city people trying to live in the country; it just didn't work.

"You see, for us, Belfast was always home, especially the Shankill. Belfast with its River Lagan, Black Mountain, Cave Hill and City Hall, was "home". So, on Friday afternoons we would pick Jonathan up after school and with Chara we would drive straight to Denmark Street, where we would stay until Saturday night. I have to admit, while we loved driving to Belfast on Friday afternoons, the drive back to the country on Saturday night was always very difficult.

"I learned how to smile and pretend that everything was okay even when deep inside it was anything but. When asked by locals how I was settling in and how I liked living in Rathfriland, I had learned how to choose my words very carefully as I certainly did not want to offend anyone.

"Continuing to be honest; I reached out to some of the more down to earth women in the church and built good relationships and friendships with them, and in so doing it helped me feel more connected not only with them and with the church, but it also helped me feel a bit more connected with Rathfriland-on-the-hill, as they called it. It was my way of at least making the effort to try and change how I felt about living there. But every weekend we just kept going back to Belfast, which I suppose didn't help. It also didn't help that things were happening back in Denmark Street that kept us attached to the street we had left for Bible College.

"I remember that in July 1981, street parties were being held all over the UK to celebrate the Royal Wedding of Prince Charles and Diana. The people of Denmark Street showed their loyalty to the Royal Family by arranging their own street party, with tables down the middle of the street covered in Union Jacks, and with plenty of food and games for the kids. It was something we knew we couldn't miss, and so we drove 'home' for the street party. It's just the way it was! If it was happening there, we wanted to be there, but then not everything that happened in Denmark Street was as joyous as a street party for the Royal Wedding.

"A few months after joining in with the festivities Denmark Street was impacted once again by violence with the murder of another one of our friends and neighbours. He was William McCullough, known to everyone as Bucky. He had lived in the same street as Jackie in Brown Square, and like most other 'Brown Square millionaires', he had also made the move to Denmark Street. Bucky had married Barbara Martin, whose mother owned the fish & chip shop that Jackie had taken me to for our plate of chips with two forks. Bucky and Barbara were raising a family together right there, but that was to change.

"One morning in 1981, Bucky dropped one of his children off at a pre-school nursery just a few yards from his home. It's my understanding that when he walked back across the street to where his car had been parked outside his own home, two men on a motorbike pulled up beside him. Bucky could see that at least one of the men was armed and he knew they were there for him. He was carrying his youngest child in his arms. It seems that the gunman permitted Bucky to put the child into the back seat of his car, at which point he opened fire hitting Bucky several times and killing him right in front of his own home. Bucky left a wife, four young daughters and two young sons. The area had lost another one of its sons. We were returning to Denmark Street once again, only this time it was for the funeral of one of our friends.

"We might have left Denmark Street and the Shankill community, but they had not left us. Later that year during Christmas season, we attended a convention service in the Ulster Temple, another Elim Church in Belfast. I remember Pastor Eric McComb, the superintendent for the Elim Churches in Ireland, calling Jackie aside during the break between meetings and speaking privately with him. Several minutes later, Jackie came to where I was sitting and told me that the leadership in Ballysillan Elim, a church in the Shankill community not far from Denmark Street, wanted Jackie to pastor the church. I could feel my heart beat at the very idea of it and was totally delighted, but even more so when Jackie told me he had already accepted the invitation. We were so excited with the thought that we were on our way back to Belfast, back to the Shankill Road, to the place we call home.

"The people in Rathfriland and Moneyslane were by no means happy to see us go, but they gave us a great send-off, and so within a few months we were inducted into Ballysillan Elim Church. That was April 1982 and was also the month our third child was born, our second daughter Paula, named after Paul, Jackie's favourite Apostle. I remember Jackie saying, "Every time we move, we have a child," to which I responded, "Well, stop moving then"! And it worked! We stopped moving, and we stopped having children.

"So, we moved back to the Shankill and have been here ever since. We both remained committed to Ballysillan Elim Church for the next ten years, and have remained committed to the Shankill and beyond for 40 years."

Outside Rathfriland Elim after 2½ years

Chapter 6

Our Home was a Stranger's Refuge

Kathleen continues: "I loved our new home in Ballysillan. I seriously felt like a proper housewife again, living in my own home looking after my own family. I could look out from our living room window and see across the city of Belfast and beyond. I could even see the Mountains of Mourne in County Down about 40 miles south of Belfast. It was especially beautiful at night when the lights of the city lit up the night-time sky. The house we moved to belonged to Ballysillan Elim, but I felt like I was home for the first time in five years, and that's how it was for the next ten years. It was everything a woman would want in a home, with a garden at the front and a larger garden at the back where the children could play safely with each other and with friends they would bring home after school and at weekends. I seriously felt so honoured and blessed to live there, and honoured to host several guest speakers over the years, most of whom were amazing. They included pastor and singer, Ray Beavan from Wales, Pastor Alex Tee from Scotland, members of Elim's National Youth Team from England, and several others during those ten years.

"But not all guest speakers who stayed did so with the grace and courtesy of Ray and Alex.

"I remember one speaker from the USA who stayed with us for two weeks. It was the longest two weeks of my life that brought sheer personal tension and stress. I felt like I was looking after a man who had never grown up.

"Most days he would lounge around my home in his dressing gown until he was ready to leave to preach. Then whatever time he would arrive back, he would have a bath with care in the world about anyone else in the house needing the toilet before bedtime, especially when there were children. Smelling fresh he would put on his jammies and dressing gown, and would then spread himself out on our sofa and say, "Kathleen the Queen, I'd like one of those Ulster Fry's; that included two fried eggs, bacon, sausages, potato bread and soda bread and of course tea.

"Oh, the number of times I would bite my lip when I heard him call me 'Kathleen the Queen,' I knew immediately he was looking for something. My reaction was not only 'not Christian-like,' but I also knew it also wasn't Kathleen-like. Thankfully, none of our other guests were anything like our one friend from Tulsa.

"Jackie then one day told me he had invited the Lord Mayor of Belfast to our home for tea. I had never had a Lord Mayor visit us in our home before! How do you host a Lord Mayor? What would I serve him, and what would I serve it on? Would he take his tea in a mug, or should I play it safe and give him tea in a cup with a saucer? I put some of these questions to Jackie, to which he replied, "Stop worrying! It's only Sammy Wilson!" Well, Sammy Wilson or not, he was the Lord Mayor of Belfast and I needed to make sure that I treated him with the respect that the office commanded.

"It was on a Sunday night after the evening service, that the Mayor was coming for tea. Jackie had invited him to present a trophy to someone in the Haddock family who had a snooker competition that Jackie had arranged, between the Haddocks and some of the men in the church. Well, the Haddocks won, but Jackie always said there was something fishy about it! (Sorry…Jackie told me to say that!) Anyway, Jackie took a lot of abuse from some of the church people for 'desecrating the service' by having such a presentation, but this was his way of reaching out to men in the community by organising competitions and presenting the winning trophies in church because it got the men into church, including their family members and their friends, but for some, it was a step too far.

"Well, other than the voice of discontent, the service went as Jackie had hoped. Besides the normal church people, the Haddocks had turned out in force, and the Lord Mayor, Sammy Wilson, spoke quite well and made the presentation. After the service, the Mayor came to our home as planned. He pulled up outside our front door in his chauffeur-driven limousine. Still wearing his Gold Chain of Office, he came into our home where I had sandwiches and cakes ready, besides tea that was served with a cup and saucer of the best quality that I could find. For several years now, and up to this present day, Sammy Wilson has been an MP in the British Parliament in London. His father, the late Pastor Sandy Wilson, was for many years pastor of Bangor Elim and was also Superintendent of the Elim Churches in Ireland.

"However, having our home open was not just about preachers and Lord Mayors, but our home also became a refuge and a hiding place for troubled youth. We had seen the church grow in many ways, but the biggest change for me personally was when Jackie started to bring a whole group of young people from the church to our home on Sunday nights. In fact, this became a regular Sunday night after church activity, and it went on for decades! While Jackie was with the young people, playing games like Balderdash and Trivial Pursuit and a game called Mafia, I was making tea and putting out the snacks, but I have to say I loved those Sunday nights. I became like a mother to other people's children; well, at least that's how I felt. Making tea and pouring out drinks, putting out buns and biscuits soon became my norm on Sunday nights; but those young people were worth every biscuit and drink.

"Sometimes we went to other homes on Sunday nights, and I loved that as well, because mixing after church and playing various games is what helped us bond so well with the young people. The youth group grew to the point where we had to build an extension to the back of the church that was used as a Youth Club, but also for midweek meetings. The church was growing so much that we had to knock down walls and extend the front section of the building to get more chairs in. More chairs meant more people, and more people meant more hospitality and more socialising, but I loved it.

"Jackie and I both loved it in Ballysillan Elim, although we did have our moments, especially one that almost finished Jackie's ministry. But before getting into that, I should say that by this time, Jackie was known as Jack, or as Pastor Jack, rather than Jackie. The change from Jackie to Jack came about when Jackie began to feel that Jack sounded more masculine than Jackie. So, while most people call him Jack, I still call him Jackie! Anyway, there was one situation that almost ended Jackie's ministry as a pastor, and at the same time, my role as a pastor's wife. Without going into the details, because I don't know them all, one of the church elders turned against Jackie to such an extent, that he decided it was pointless to continue as pastor of Ballysillan Elim. So, he sat down and wrote a letter of resignation to Pastor Eric McComb, the Superintendent of the Elim Movement in Ireland at that time.

"With tears in his eyes, he told me he was going to post the letter. I reached over to him, and as I did so, I took the letter from his hand and without even blinking, I ripped it up. It was just like that first morning in Rathfriland all over again; the pastor I was married to was wanting to walk away, but this pastor's wife had not left her home in Denmark Street, sold all her furniture, travelled up and down the length of Scotland and England for two years, used my tights as a fan belt, survived on soup with left over fried eggs mixed in, and survived on beans and toast for two years, so it would end because of a church elder. No! That was not going to happen. I told Jackie he needed to stay as pastor of the church and that I would support him as best I could.

"It was at that time that Eric phoned to tell us we had been offered the use of a bungalow with a beach at its doorstep in Millisle so we could take a break for a while. The offer, made by Mrs Norah Bradford[2], was very timely and was just what we needed at that time; so off we went to the sunny beach of Costa Del-Millisle. Within a few days we got a phone call to let us know the people in the church were angry and were asking about us, and so we returned home to a great church family welcome. Jackie stayed and continued to pastor Ballysillan Elim, not only with my support but with the support of the church and of the leadership of the Elim Movement. The church continued to grow.

Cancer takes my brother Bill

"Dealing with issues outside family is one thing, but the news came about a family member. My brother Bill had been diagnosed with cancer. Bill had never married. He had spent several years living and working in New Zealand during the 1960s, returning to Belfast around the same time The Troubles broke out in 1969. He lived with us in Brown Square before moving with us to Denmark Street in 1971. Bill was a heavy smoker, and it didn't help that he worked in a cigarette factory. Sadly, he was just into his 50s when he found out that he had cancer.

"Several months before Bill passed away, Jackie was able to pray with him and lead him to personal faith in Jesus. He started to attend Ballysillan Elim, only missing it when he wasn't feeling up to it, but his commitment to Christ and his attendance at church gave him a real sense of peace and helped him through those very difficult last months of his life. A few weeks before he passed away, Bill was taken into hospital. It broke our hearts to watch him deteriorate daily. He was no longer able to make it to church, but my sisters Marie and Sally, our brother Geordie, our parents, and Jackie, would be by his side, supporting him and supporting each other.

---

2 Norah Bradford was married to the late Robert Bradford MP, a Methodist Minister and an Ulster Unionist MP, who had been shot dead by the IRA in 1981.

"During one of Jackie's visits with him, Bill shared a dream with him Jackie in the hope that he could explain it. Let me share that dream Jackie had just preached on the subject of Heaven. Bill was not at the church to hear that message as he was in the hospital. During the message, Jackie explained that Heaven is a real place, that it really does exist. He talked about Heaven being on "the sides of the north" and explained his belief that if we could physically make it through a black hole, we would possibly discover Heaven. Now I'll leave it for others to try to work out the theology of this, but it got really interesting when soon after preaching that message, Jackie and I called at the hospital to see Bill. As soon as we entered the room, Bill immediately said he was glad to see us, as he needed to share a dream he'd had. He then went on to explain the dream as follows…

"He was standing outside a black hole he could hear singing coming from inside the black hole, and it sounded like Ballysillan Elim Church. (Jackie and I looked at each other as we both knew Bill had no idea that Jackie had just preached about Heaven, and had shared his theory of the black hole!) Bill continued… standing alongside him in the dream, were my sister Marie and me, so in Bill's dream, there was me, Marie and Bill, standing outside a black hole. Bill then explained that at one point, a little white bird with blue wings came hopping out of the black hole towards us, but it stopped and looked up at him. It then turned and hopped back towards the black hole, but it then stopped and looked back at Bill as if to suggest it wanted him to follow it into the black hole where the singing was coming from.

"He looked at Marie and me and asked if we were going with him, but Marie said, "No, Bill, it's not our time yet; we'll be coming later." Bill then said that at that point, he turned towards the little bird and then followed it into the black hole. He said the further he walked inside the black hole, the louder the singing became and that he felt such an amazing sense of peace. Having shared his dream with us, he then asked if we had any idea what the dream meant. Jackie then began to explain to Bill how he had only just preached about Heaven and that he believed this was God's way of showing Bill that soon he would be going home and that he had nothing to fear as he was ready to go and be with Jesus. Within a few days, and with several of us around his bed, Bill peacefully drifted off in his sleep. But it didn't end there, let's see how the dream unfolds...

"My parents decided to cremate Bill's body so that later his ashes could be placed alongside them in their grave when they would pass away. In the meantime, they had arranged for his ashes to be buried close to their holiday caravan in Millisle, where they stayed many weekends and for most of the summer weeks. The owner of the caravan park, Mrs Mitchell, had suggested burying Bill's ashes in a spot close to and in clear view of my parent's caravan. The place she suggested was at the foot of a little bush right next to a wire fence that was no more than four feet high. Jackie did a short service for the family and a few friends who had gathered. As we walked towards the little bush, Mrs. Mitchell said, "The reason I suggested this fence is because this is where the birds land each day, and I come along and feed them at this bush."

"When Jackie finished the service, the groundsman began to fill in the hole. As he was covering the casket with soil, he spoke and said, "In all my years, I have not seen soil as black as this." Jackie and I looked at each other because we both knew what was happening. This was Bill's dream being fulfilled in the natural, and was a clear sign to us that his dream was also being fulfilled in the supernatural. First of all, there was the bush where the little birds landed each day, and secondly, there was a black hole into which Bill's ashes were being placed. But what about the singing? Bill had said he could hear singing that sounded like Ballysillan Elim. Well, on the other side of the four-foot-high fence and right beside the bush where Bill's ashes were being buried was another Elim Church. It was Millisle Elim, where they sang the same songs and where the singing was very much like the singing in Ballysillan Elim. It was just like Bill had said, the black hole, the bird, and the singing. When Jackie shared this with Mrs Mitchell and with the family while having tea afterwards, there wasn't a dry eye in the room.

"My reason for sharing the above story about Bill is because he was a very special brother who left us too soon, but thankfully he made his peace with God. I know he's with the Lord in Heaven, and that someday we'll be together again, including Marie, who was also in the dream, and our other sister Sally, who after Bill's death, came to personal faith in Jesus. I also share the story to show that none of us are immune to trouble and heartache and that while Jackie was having to give time to deal with issues in the church, we also had to cope with the sickness and loss of Bill. But we pushed through and continued to serve God in Ballysillan."

Two carrots put before us

Kathleen and I remained in Ballysillan Elim, where we continued to lead the church forward and touch the community around us for the remainder of the 1980s. We really felt that God's hand was upon us as a church, as a family, and as a husband-and-wife team who were dedicated to each other and to serving Him and the community. Yes, there were some issues and what church has not got issues – even if you don't see them. But things were generally good. However, after seven years of being in Ballysillan and having been Youth Director for Elim in Ireland for several years, Kathleen and I began to talk about other churches and the possibility of one day moving on to another church. It's not that we wanted to or were planning to; we just chatted about possibilities and the what-ifs, and wondered where we would like to go if we ever did decide to move on.

We talked about Bangor Elim, as I'd got to know a number of its young people and their youth leaders at several youth events, and got on quite well with them. We also talked about Carrick Elim, but mainly because a number of our friends were attending there, Philip and Carol Griffiths, and Desi and Elizabeth Burgess, who've been mentioned several times as our friends who drove us to our honeymoon in Portrush. But, we also thought about Carrick Elim because Carrickfergus was a place we both said that we would like to live and raise our children, but also because it had a castle, whereas Bangor didn't! However, all of this was only small talk; it was nothing serious. Our focus remained on Ballysillan.

However, one day our phone rang, and it was Pastor Eric McComb, our Superintendent. It was totally out of the blue and totally unexpected. He called to say that Bangor Elim was becoming available, as the pastor there was moving, but also to say that the church leadership in Bangor was inviting me to consider becoming its pastor. I was completely blown away. I felt so honoured and excited at the prospect, but Kathleen and I needed time to talk this over together and to pray about it. We both loved the idea, but there was something that just didn't sit right. Neither of us had a peace about it. I can assure you that we both tried to manufacture even a sense of peace, but no matter how much we tried, peace kept eluding us.

Pastor Eric McComb gave us two weeks to talk it over and pray about it, but we took three weeks and even then, I didn't have it in me to contact him because I really didn't want to be saying, "No." Not able to hold off any longer, Eric finally called me. He was surprised that Kathleen and I had decided to turn down such an opportunity. This was our number one dream church that we'd been offered, and yet we turned it down. We did so because we both knew in our hearts that it just wasn't right for us at that time.

So, having put that one behind us, we focused again on Ballysillan Elim, but within a very short space of time, Eric called again. This time he told me that Carrickfergus Elim was without a pastor and that the leadership there was inviting me to be their pastor. Wow! I was totally blown away because this was the second church on my list of two churches that I'd want to pastor if ever I felt it was time to move on. However, in an instant, I was able to say no and turn the invitation down because I did not want Kathleen and I to go through the same turmoil we'd just gone through with Bangor.

The crazy thing was the fact that we had no idea why we turned down those two churches, and so for a while, we were left wondering what might have been. However, it wasn't long before we got some answers, and those answers came through Belfast's most popular newspaper, the Belfast Telegraph.

Kathleen shares: "It was just another normal day. Jackie had been out visiting. The kids had been to school. I had made dinner as normal, and when dinner was over, Jackie went into the kitchen to wash the dishes while I read the newspaper. It was then I noticed an advert showing that an old cinema on the Shankill Road was for sale, and I remember shouting out loud, "JACKIE, THE STADIUM'S FOR SALE!"

"At that point, Jackie came walking into the living room with a cup and a tea towel in his hands. He took a brief look at the advert and went back to doing the dishes in the kitchen while I continued reading the paper. That was it. No waving of hands or arms, just no response. However, I had no idea as to how much that moment would change our lives, because that was a moment that would lead to the launch of a major community organisation that would touch the lives of many, both old and young; that would lead to the launch of an amazing church that would reach many across Belfast and beyond, but more importantly for me, was that it would lead to the birth and development of Hobby Horse Playgroup, that was to become my life."

Kathleen's words, "The Stadium's for sale" kept resonating in my mind throughout the night and the following day. I couldn't shift them. Her words echoed like the kind of call that caused Abraham to leave his comfort zone in Harran with the urge to follow that call, not knowing where it would take him. There was nothing at that time that was stronger than the urge inside of me to find out why The Stadium was for sale and who was selling it. After several phone calls and several typed letters, besides a whole lot of praying, within just a few months, and against all the odds and some serious opposition, we managed to purchase the old Stadium, turning it into a youth and community outreach facility, calling it Stadium Youth & Community Centre. We opened in September 1989, but it was only as we moved forward in the coming weeks and months, and as we saw how things were developing, that we remembered Bangor and Carrick, and only then did we know why we had said no to those two amazing offers and amazing churches. We continued in Ballysillan Elim Church for another three years, where I continued to pastor while also fulfilling the role of Director of Stadium Youth and Community Centre. Kathleen continued to be the wonderful pastor's wife, while at the same time leading and developing her amazing Hobby Horse Playgroup. The new outreach centre on the Shankill Road opened opportunities to reach out to the wider community in new and innovative ways, enabling us to put into practice the words of Paul when he said, *"By all means, save some"* (1 Corinthians 9:22).

The Old Stadium secured

We developed a community outreach project that would touch the lives of many, which included training and employment opportunities for the wider community. We did so in partnership with the Elim Movement and with what was called the ACE Scheme (Action for Community Employment), a government-funded employment scheme that provided full-time staff and enabled us to develop youth activities and youth programmes.

The Old Stadium renovated

While my main focus was on reaching young people, especially young men being recruited by local paramilitary groups and being caught up in drug abuse and criminality, Kathleen's focus was on children, which led to the creation of an amazing pre-school playgroup. Kathleen explains how this happened:

"It was great to see Jackie developing the Stadium and its activities, but the new centre also gave me the opportunity to do something I had only ever dreamed of doing, and that was to run a pre-school playgroup; a dream that I was able to fulfil by the founding and launch of Hobby Horse Playgroup in September 1989. I remember seeing a room within the centre that would be big enough to hold sixteen children and three members of staff. That was all I needed to get me going.

"Initially, we were all volunteers, but then, with the help of the ACE Scheme, we were able to provide employment. The only problem was, that you could only be on the ACE Scheme for one year. Then you had to register as unemployed again for a year, after which you could come back onto the ACE Scheme for another year. So, for several years, I personally was employed as the Playgroup Manager for a year, then I would register as unemployed for a year, work voluntary and then go back onto the ACE Scheme for another year. This is how it was for many years until we finally managed to secure funds to properly employ playgroup staff.

"Hobby Horse Playgroup became a massive success overnight, and it continues to be a huge success to this very day. For over 30 years, we have provided pre-school education in our morning playgroup for 3-year-olds and have provided afternoon childcare in our after-school Butterfly Club for children with special needs, mostly with autism. During these years, we have catered for around 1,000 children in total, besides providing additional support to parents and families. Most of these children have come from the Shankill community, many from Denmark Street and the redeveloped Brown Square area.

"One of the many satisfying things over the years for me personally, was seeing many of those who had attended Hobby Horse as children, become parents themselves and then return with their own children later so that they also could attend Hobby Horse Playgroup. We just loved connecting with children and their families, and although our main focus was always on those families within our own community, that did not prevent us from accepting children from other communities, regardless of where they came from and regardless of their religious, political or ethnic background.

"Neither did it prevent us from reaching out to build relationships with similar childcare projects in other parts of Belfast, both Protestant and Catholic. I had the privilege of being part of a lobby group that consisted of community childcare practitioners and of team leaders from various funding organisations. Together we would meet with politicians and key stakeholders in the hope of improving the provision and quality of childcare across Belfast, but I have to admit that my main focus was always Hobby Horse Playgroup and the Butterfly Club. I lived for those children."

Hobby Horse Playgroup

As a hen gathers her children

While thinking of Kathleen and her work with children, I'm reminded of the time when Jesus wept over the City of Jerusalem and its people. While sitting on the Mount of Olives, He was looking towards the walled city with the Temple at its centre taking pride of place. As Jesus looked towards the city, He said, "Oh Jerusalem, Jerusalem, I have longed to gather your children together, as a hen gathers her chicks under her wings." In thinking of these words, I can almost hear God say, "Kathleen, that's what I've called and gifted you to do; to gather the children of Belfast under your wings, wings that provide cover and protection for many children, near and far." These included children from her home community in Denmark Street; from across the Shankill and from the Falls communities, and of course her own children she'd given birth to; not forgetting many young people being welcomed into an open home for somewhere to go in times of personal need and of community tensions, where they would feel real Christian love in a safe place. However, Kathleen's love for children was not confined to Belfast, as she explains next:

Kathleen says, "I've always known that my gifting and calling was to reach out to and provide cover for children and for young people brought up in the Shankill community, but sometimes my heartstrings were stretched beyond our own community and even beyond the city of Belfast. For example, I remember one morning in 1991, we were having breakfast while watching the early morning news as we normally did. The BBC was running a series of special reports from Albania. I was glued to the TV as images of children's hospitals and orphanages appeared on the screen, and I was horrified by what I saw – children who had nothing, not even clothes on their backs.

"Most of the children were completely naked. I think the BBC showed it as it was, perhaps to shock the world into what was happening. The children were lying on beds without mattresses, just the bare spring to lie on and not even a blanket to provide at least some comfort. There was no dignity afforded to those children, as their images were put on public display for all to see; but not only were they naked, but it was also quite apparent that these children had not been served a proper meal for weeks. All I could see were naked and hungry children, and I began to weep as I put my unfinished breakfast down on the table.

"Through my tears and my sobs, I began to complain to Jackie about the tragic conditions faced by these children in Albania. I complained about a world that ignored the plight of these children, and about governments, including our own, saying that they could do something if they wanted to. Within a few short minutes, I had complained about everyone and anyone who either allowed these conditions to exist or were remaining passive and quiet while these children were literally dying of starvation or freezing to death. But the only one who was listening was Jackie. Suddenly he spoke back to me and said, "Why don't you stop your crying and do something about it?" Me? I thought I was doing enough. I was complaining. Surely that was enough!

"I was getting our own children ready for school that morning and was preparing myself for work with the children at Hobby Horse Playgroup.

Here I was, watching children on the television in Albania who were a long way off from my reality in Belfast, and now the challenge is laid before me to stop crying about the plight of these children and to actually do something about it! But what could I do?

"Well, knowing that I needed to respond to the challenge, and with God's help, I stretched out those wings like a mother hen gathering her chicks and reached out to those children in Albania. I left home that morning with the determination that even though I was living and working within the Shankill community, I was going to do something to help those children in the orphanages in Albania, although at that moment, I had no idea what that would be. However, what started with an emotional reaction to a news item, became the heart of conversations over the next number of days and weeks, until eventually, I had pulled together teams of volunteers who would help make something happen.

"We began raising finances and supplies. I secured the loan of two 40 ft trucks and containers with two drivers in each truck, and within a matter of weeks, I was leading a team of seven from Belfast to Albania with the containers loaded with food, clothes, medical supplies, blankets and so much more. Jackie's challenge helped me recognise that it was not enough to just sit and tearfully watch television as it showed images of hurting children, but the greater response was to actually get up and do something, and that's precisely what I and others did. We got up, and we went to Albania.

"Along with me and the containers filled were four drivers: Stephen Robinson, a leader in one of our Elim churches and the owner of one of the trucks; Stephen Matthews, an Elim pastor, Cameron Crawford, who at that time was pastoring alongside Jackie and was also helping manage Stadium Youth & Community Centre, but who sadly passed away during the writing of this book. Then there was Brian Ward, who was a driver for one of the haulage companies that donated one of the trucks for the mission. Finally, there were two female companions who had helped pull it all together: Carolyn McComb, who at that time attended Ballysillan Elim Church, and Linda Martin who was Jackie's Personal Assistant at the centre.

"So, within several weeks from seeing the plight of children in Albanian orphanages, containers were on their way from the Shankill community to Tirana, Albania's capital city. They travelled down through Scotland to Dover in England, where they got the ferry to France, then driving to Italy, where they met us girls who had flown to Bari. We stayed overnight in a hotel in Bari, although two of the drivers stayed with the trucks and joined us the following morning for breakfast. With everyone now together and on board, we drove to Brindisi in Italy, where we caught an overnight ferry to Igoumenitsa, Greece. Driving up through Greece, we slept in the trucks as they travelled through the Greek mountains (except for those driving, of course). We arrived at the Albanian border during the night, where we had to bribe the border guard to let us into Albania.

"A few cigarettes that we'd been advised to bring with us for this very purpose, and a pen, were quite sufficient to get us over the border. No sooner had we entered Albania, driving along country roads and through villages when it became apparent that people were taking notice of us and of the trucks with their massive containers. The people had obviously known that trucks like ours were bringing supplies to orphanages and hospitals, yet the sad reality was that the trucks were driving straight through the villages where families were just as needy as those in the orphanages.

"Our hearts were broken by what we saw, and while we gave away some bars of chocolate and other bits and pieces as we drove along the roads and through the villages, we remained focused on our main reason for being there. We were to connect with a Mission Team that was working from a warehouse distributing supplies to the hospitals and orphanages in Tirana. When we finally arrived in Tirana, we drove to the main square but had no idea that lots of people gathered in the square at nights where they would just sit around. Apparently, this is what they did every night! They just gathered at the square because there was nothing else to do in Tirana.

"As we drove into the square, we immediately became the focus of attention. People were waving at us and greeting us, but we knew we couldn't stop, so we kept moving until we got to the hotel where we'd booked to stay for one night. This was a hotel where we had rump soup for supper before making our first contact with the Mission Team from Brazil that was distributing supplies to the orphanages. The following day we made our way to the distribution warehouse, where we were welcomed by the team leader. We were encountered by many locals trying to see what we had and what they could get. Some of the locals volunteered to help us unload the trucks. We left everything with the Mission Team, who assured us that everything we had brought would be delivered to the appropriate and most needy orphanages.

"Having left the supplies with the Mission Team, we drove back to the Greek border where we once again stayed overnight in the mountains. The next morning, we made our way back through Greece to Igoumenitsa, where we caught a ferry back to Brindisi, Italy, and then back to Bari. Here, we girls caught a flight back to Belfast while the men continued driving through Italy and France, back into England and Scotland until they finally arrived back in Belfast. It was an amazing journey that started in our home several months earlier, while watching the early morning news on BBC. We knew we had done something together that was so worthwhile. God only knows how many children and families were helped.

"Sadly, sometime after returning home, Linda Martin died under very tragic circumstances. We remember Linda and Cameron Crawford with great fondness."

Chapter 7

Suffer the Little Children

When Kathleen got back from Albania, it was back to her main focus, the children of Hobby Horse Playgroup. At that time, the playgroup was still in a little back room in the old Stadium Centre. They didn't have much, but they had enough determination and know-how to give the children a great learning experience during their time at Hobby Horse. Besides the little back room, they were also able to use the main hall that was mainly used for sports and other activities. There the children were able to play in the open space with their prams and bikes. A room with some toys, a few tables and chairs, and some space to move around was all that was required because life back then was much simpler and less complicated than it is today. At times though, it was just as challenging and just as devastating, as Kathleen explains next.

"We've had many great success stories of how much the children benefitted during their time with us, and of staff members not only adding to their experience but also adding to their qualifications in childcare. That helped us become one of the most successful preschool playgroups within the city of Belfast. However, there were not always good news stories, because sadly, we experienced several tragedies that affected our children and their families. As we were located on the Shankill Road, we went through some very dark days due to Northern Ireland's conflict: a conflict that not only impacted on the lives of our children in Hobby Horse, but also on the lives of young people we worked directly with from within the community.

Some attended our church, and several were in our home on Sunday nights and at other times.

"In February 1992, Jackie told the leadership in Ballysillan Elim that our time there had come to an end after ten years. They were shocked! They had no idea we were even thinking that way, but Jackie began to feel the pressure of trying to pastor the church while at the same time leading and developing the new centre on the Shankill Road. He even brought two other pastors onto the leadership team, Cameron Crawford and David Hamilton, to help with the preaching and the visitations. Finally, it reached the point where Jackie felt he had to choose between the church and the new outreach centre.

"After genuinely praying about it and chatting with me about the possibilities, Jackie chose the centre over the church. His main reason for doing so was that the Stadium, as we called it, was connecting him with the community in ways he had not experienced as pastor of a church. Some of those he was connecting with through the centre were young men caught up in a lifestyle of drugs. They were also being recruited by the local paramilitaries who were using them, controlling them, and beating or shooting them. I remember Jackie publicly stating that the increase in drugs coming into our community would lead to addictions and death on a scale equal to what was happening in Dublin at that time. He was criticised by some so-called community leaders, who accused him of scaremongering. I wonder what those same so-called community leaders are saying about the drug problem within our community today! These were things I had to watch and listen to without getting involved, because my focus was the playgroup and the children.

"However, within a few weeks of announcing to the church that we were leaving Ballysillan Elim, we faced one of our greatest tragedies ever, one that broke both of our hearts and still hurts to this day. It was on a Monday night in February 1992. I was at home that night while

Jackie had gone to visit someone in the hospital. The house phone rang. I picked it up, thinking it would be someone looking for Jackie. The person asked for Jackie, but there was a panic in their voice that concerned me. When I told them that Jackie was not at home, the person then said to me, "Andrew Johnston's been shot dead."

"I remember feeling numb. I had no idea what to say. I began to cry. Andrew was one of those I referred to above, who we'd got to know and love. Our Youth Fellowship was meeting at church that night. Jonathan and Chara were both there, while Paula was at home with me. There was nothing I could do, and I couldn't get in touch with Jackie, so I had to sit and wait until he got home. As soon as I saw the car pull up, I ran out to meet him before he came into the house. I could hardly speak as I was so emotional, but I did manage to say enough to let him know that young Andrew had been shot dead.

"I could immediately see the shock and anger on his face. Jackie got straight back into the car and drove off in the direction of the church. I didn't see him until later that night, but when he did come home, he was in such a state. We both sat and cried and were totally bewildered that this could happen to one of our young men, who one week earlier had cried at the news of Catholics being gunned down and killed in a betting shop in Belfast. Now this young man lay dead in a senseless act of retaliation for those very murders that caused him to weep. So many pointless deaths happened, many of whom were young people and children, and to most people, Andrew was just another one; but to us he was Andrew Johnston, one of our very own young people. I felt like I had lost a child."

Kathleen explains the loss of Andrew Johnston so well. I might have been his pastor, but Kathleen had given him drinks and biscuits and welcomed him into our home several times with other young people from the church. We had watched him grow from when he was seven years old, into a young man who was honourable in all his ways. I remember when we first arrived at Ballysillan Elim that we saw Yvonne in church, and we immediately recognised her from our days back in Brown Square. She was one of the first in the church we visited, and when we did, she told us she was a single mum. She then introduced us to her little red-haired, freckled-faced, Andrew. He was only seven and at primary school.

Andrew was Yvonne's only child. When he was 11 years old, he committed his young life to follow Jesus, and was baptised in water when he was 14. He became quite a shining light within the church youth group. He was also a friend to Jonathan and Chara, along with his girlfriend, Julie. Everyone got on well with Andrew, but now, with two bullets in his chest, he lay dead in a video shop where he had worked part-time, only 50 yards from our church, where his friends who loved him had been gathering in the youth group.

Our hearts were broken. We even questioned if it was now the right time for us to leave the church, although we knew in our hearts that we should still move on as planned. And so, one of the last things we did before leaving Ballysillan was to reach out to comfort Andrew's mother, Yvonne, and his stepfather Stevie, and other members of the family, and to officiate at the funeral. Thousands came out to show their respect and their repulsion at the murder of such an innocent young man and show their support for his family. Kathleen says, "One of the last things our own children did before leaving Ballysillan Elim, was to walk behind the coffin of their young friend Andrew Johnston," which was true; but sadly, Andrew would not be the last.

Suffering spans the decades

Being right at the heart of Northern Ireland's conflict was something I had learned to cope with. But one of the darkest periods we went through as a community, that impacted the lives of many families,

including the lives of children across the community and those children
who attended Hobby Horse, was the 'Loyalist Feud' that broke out
on the Shankill Road during the year 2000. This was a bloody and
murderous feud between Protestant terror groups who turned against
each other. In just a few days, 11 men within our community lay dead;
their families thrust into darkness, despair and grief. Many others had
been shot and wounded, and dozens of families, including children,
were forcefully driven out from their homes and evicted from certain
parts of our community, where they had lived for years. Unfortunately,
Hobby Horse Playgroup did not go unscathed during those painful
and tragic weeks. Kathleen picks it up from here:

"Like most women in our community, I felt so helpless. We had often
seen what happened when men fell out with each other, but this was
different. I don't ever remember seeing this kind of fallout before. They
called it a feud. Its impact was sudden and devastating. The fear across
the community could be felt by everyone, and not even Hobby Horse
Playgroup could escape, as many of our children were directly affected.
Some of their fathers, grandfathers, and other family members were
actively caught up on one side or other of the feud.

"Prior to the feud, the location of Hobby Horse was not a problem for
any of these children, but everything changed as the feud spread across
the entire community, becoming more vicious and bloodier. We saw
fear like we had never seen before, especially on the faces of many of
our children within the playgroup. Sadly, some of the children who
came from the Upper Shankill were prevented from returning to Hobby
Horse due to our location within the Lower Shankill community. It
might not have mattered before, but it mattered now.

"Such was the mayhem and fear created by the feud that many families
had to flee their homes without even a moment's notice. They did so
with nowhere permanent to go, moving in wherever possible, be it
with family members or with friends, but in many cases only taking

what they could carry or what they could fit inside their car. Opposing paramilitary members, responsible for evicting people from their homes, would take hold of the vacant homes and either set them on fire with the furniture still inside, or they would throw the furniture onto the street and put someone else into the home who had been evicted from another part of the community.

"I remember one day a woman who was extremely upset, came to our home looking for Jackie to help her. She and her family were being evicted from their home, but they were one of the "lucky ones" as they'd been given two hours to leave, but she had no idea what to do with her furniture. My heart went out to her, and so I said to Jackie that we could move the playgroup into the church hall, and use the vacated space to store furniture until they were able to collect it - although I had no idea that the feud would go on for several weeks.

"That same day and night, we moved all our playgroup equipment, tables, chairs, toys, bikes and prams, into the church hall, thinking it might be for a few days, not knowing it would be for several weeks. It meant that we would have to put all the playgroup equipment away at the weekends and then set it back out on Mondays. But we were happy to do this as we knew that not only would it prevent furniture from being destroyed, but it would possibly save lives. It also enabled Jackie, supported by others, to work with other families who were also being evicted and to bring their furniture to the playgroup where it would remain until the families had been rehoused and were able to come back and reclaim it. Some of the items being stored were fridges with food still inside, such was the haste in vacating their homes. The feud was so severe that it left its mark not only on our community and on many families, but also on the lives of our children in Hobby Horse."

Not all suffering was Troubles related

Not all of the tragedies we faced as a family, as a church, and as a community outreach were related to Northern Ireland's conflict or the feud we had experienced within the Shankill, but some were down to more personal circumstances. In the following paragraphs, Kathleen shares one of her most painful moments while at Hobby Horse playgroup:

"It was November 2006, and only four weeks away from Christmas. Madison Bothwell was only four years of age. He had been with us in Hobby Horse for his pre-school year and had not long left when he, along with his father and his grandmother, all died together as a result of a fire in their home. His father, also called Jackie, was friendly with my Jackie. He had played football for the New Life Young Men's Football Team; he had travelled to Scotland with them and had been attending church at times.

"The sudden and tragic loss of Jackie Bothwell, along with his mother and young Madison, sent shockwaves across the Shankill, and because of the connection with New Life City Church and with Hobby Horse, Jackie had the responsibility of conducting the joint funeral service of all three. It was so heart-breaking for so many of us who knew and loved them, but it also had such an impact on the staff at Hobby Horse who had worked with Madison during his pre-school year.

"We cried together as a staff at the loss of one of our little ones. I also called several times to the home of his mother Lisa to try and comfort her; and provide her with some support. Hobby Horse later opened an outside play area for both the playgroup and the Butterfly Club that was funded by the Department for Communities in Northern Ireland. When we formally opened the play area, we tearfully dedicated it to the memory of our little Madison. Of course, our thoughts and prayers were also with his father Jackie and his grandmother who died alongside Madison in the fire, and with the family circle that was grieving so much.

"The suffering of children comes in many forms, whether it's personal illnesses or the break-up of parents and the end of family life. Sometimes it's the tragic loss of a parent, as was the case of one of the children who attended the Butterfly Club whose father would drop him off with us every day. The little boy, like every other child in the Butterfly Club, had additional needs. His father would leave him with us at 2 pm each day and would pick him up again around 4.30 pm. Everything seemed okay until, one day, the father and the boy arrived just like they'd done so many other times. There was nothing that looked different that day and nothing that caused us to be concerned. Everything looked and felt normal, but sadly the father did not return to pick the child up at the end of the day.

"Without going into detail, we had no idea that the father had been experiencing personal difficulties that would sadly lead to his untimely death. For us, this was heart-breaking, as we felt deeply for the child and his family. It was also a huge challenge to us, as it made us realise that our work should not conclude by engaging only with the child who attends Hobby Horse Playgroup or the Butterfly Club. But we should also be reaching out to the wider family to provide whatever additional support we could offer. This is something we now do through our weekly Parents and Toddlers Group, and our Parents Support Group, and by working in partnership with GLOW (Giving Life Opportunities to Women) where parents are encouraged to participate in programmes and in a number of activities, that offer personal development and additional support whenever required."

Kathleen has always understood that when Jesus said, *"Suffer the little children,"* that He was not suggesting that children should suffer because in the language of that day, it simply meant "allow" (the little children to come to Me). Adults should be welcoming to children and should show patience towards them; but the fact is, children do suffer in this world, and they do so for many reasons. By helping the parent where possible, we believe we are also helping the child, but then there are those times when, no matter how much we want to help, all we can offer is our love and prayers, and then leave the person in God's hands. This causes me to think of one more little child to whom I had the privilege of being pastor, but Kathleen will share from her perspective, as she likewise had the privilege of spending much time with this little girl whether in the hospital or her home. Kathleen writes:

"Dempsey was not one of our children at Hobby Horse but was a little three-year-old Scottish girl who was first brought to church by her mum Lynn and her dad Robert who are both Scottish. It is so sad for any parent to lose a child at any time, including miscarriage and stillbirth, but to lose a child you raised and had prepared for school is any parent's worst nightmare. Little Dempsey had been diagnosed with cancer when she was only five, and for three years, little Dempsey, her mum and dad and their family battled against this horrible disease. At one point in 2016, Dempsey, with the help of an amazing medical profession both at home and in the USA, and with God's help, went into remission. We were all so excited as it really looked like Dempsey had beaten cancer, but sadly within a few months, it was back with a vengeance.

"Finally, in January 2017, with her mum Lynn by her side as always, little Dempsey passed away peacefully in hospital. Robert and Lynn have shared how Dempsey remained compassionate and courageous throughout her illness and that they both took great comfort in knowing that their little Dempsey has gone to be with Jesus. For such a young child who had gone through so much, Dempsey genuinely touched many lives, not only within the church but also throughout the Shankill community and across the world. We will remember Dempsey with much love and fondness, and continue to pray for her mum, Lynn, her dad Robert, and for the family that loved her and now miss her."

Chapter 8

New Season, New Challenges

Kathleen reflects briefly on our journey from one season to another:

"There was nothing I wanted more than to have a home where we could not only raise our own children, but that we'd also open it to help other people's children when the need arose. So, having an open home policy, where people could visit for a while or stay all night, if need be, was something we did from the day we were married. We went from having all-night prayer meetings to having people stay with us for several days for one reason or another. The first to stay with us were two young women from our Elim Church in Dublin who were on a mission outreach to Belfast. I remember them awakening us each morning with their singing and praying, but it was just amazing having them stay in our home. The second to stay with us was Jackie's Uncle Sandy who had been living in Australia for over 30 years, but who turned up one day completely unannounced and had nowhere to stay.

"Others included a young man from Dublin who, although he was a pastor's son, was fighting a serious drug addiction. Then there was our young friend Davy Douglas who stayed with us several times before he was murdered, and there were several others, including visiting speakers from across the UK and the USA. It's what we did. It was later in 1992, that Jackie and I bought our first home. This became not only an amazing place for us to live as a family, but just like our previous homes in Denmark Street and the church manse belonging to

Ballysillan Elim, our new home has been a shelter and a refuge for many.

"There were several times we would lift one of our children from the comfort of their bed and place them on a blanket on the floor next to us in our room so that a young person in need of refuge and support would have somewhere warm and safe to stay. I loved what we were doing, even if it meant extra cooking and being a mother to those young ones who dropped in or stayed overnight so that our home was actually an extension of our ministry. God blessed us with this new home, and we were both happy for it to be used in this way.

"Working with children and young people became the main focus of our ministry. Jackie, with his team of ACE workers and volunteers, developed programmes and activities for young people and oversaw the development of Stadium Youth and Community Centre. I, with my team of ACE Workers and volunteers focused on developing Hobby Horse Playgroup. We were both happy with this shift of focus from church to the community, believing it was a new season of ministry. Although it was different from what we were used to as normal church life, it was still a ministry. We were not being rebellious and were not being anti-church, but we had no intention of going back to the norm of pastoring another church. That's not what we were looking for, and it was certainly not what I was looking for. My focus was now Hobby Horse Playgroup."

The fact is, Kathleen and I both loved church, and we knew we still needed church, so we were looking for somewhere to make our spiritual home, a church to attend while reaching out to the community through the Centre, and especially working with young people and children. All of those years leading up to this new season and a new focus on ministry, including our years at Elim Bible College, the years at Rathfriland and Moneyslane, and of course, the ten years at Ballysillan Elim, were not wasted years. They were years of giving ourselves to the church and to the wider community, but also years of growing and maturing in ministry and life: years when we learned and experienced much more than Bible College could ever have taught or prepared us for.

With all this learning and experience, and with God's help, we felt well able to take on this new season of ministry along with whatever challenges would come with it. But, we did not possess a crystal ball and had no idea where this would lead, or what new challenges would present themselves. One thing we did know for sure was that God was still in full control, and we remained committed to serving Him. We knew Bible College had been a God thing, as was Rathfriland, Moneyslane, and Ballysillan. We also knew that God was behind the purchase of the old Stadium Cinema that began with the reading of a newspaper advert, and so we were both fully confident that God would continue to lead us through the doors we knew He had opened. However, and it's a big 'however', even though we thought we would not be pastoring a church again, unknown to us at that time, God had other thoughts.

God takes us full circle

Kathleen explains how God took us full circle from Townsend Street Elim to Bible College in 1977, and strangely back to Townsend Street Elim, 15 years later in 1992, to join the existing leadership team as one of its pastors. Kathleen shares:

"Jackie and I were okay with not pastoring a church anymore. We started to attend a few churches looking to see where we might settle. This continued for several months until one day, the pastor of Townsend Street Elim Church popped into the café in our new centre. We had called it the MILE Café, because MILE is ELIM backwards. Some people said we didn't have Elim in our name; they just weren't looking hard enough!

"Anyway, the pastor who called in was Richard McBurney. I remember seeing Richard and Jackie sitting in the café and chatting in such a way that it made me wonder what they were planning. Later that day, Jackie told me that Richard had invited him to join him on the pastoral leadership in Townsend Street Elim, but that he had said no. This is the church we had left to go to Bible College 15 years earlier. This was our home church, the building that replaced the old church building back in Brown Square. This was the same church where Jackie and I had been married in 1972, the first marriage in that building I may add, and now we were being invited back.

"Although Jackie had said no, it seemed that Richard did not take 'no' for an answer easily. He came back, not just once, but several times, and he did so until Jackie finally gave in and agreed to join the leadership team at Townsend Street Elim, but only after spending several hours being counselled and advised by Pastor Eric McComb, our then superintendent. Jackie also wanted assurances by Richard that he would be permitted to focus on developing two areas of ministry within the church, which were worship and youth outreach.

"I personally didn't need much convincing because I knew we needed a church to attend, one where we could settle and make our home, and so we both jointly agreed that Townsend Street Elim would be the church. Of course, what helped was that Jackie was not taking on the role of Leading Pastor and that I would not be required to take on the leadership role of the Women's Ministry. Everything looked okay, and so I was happy to be going back to our spiritual home where we still knew and loved many of the people."

As Kathleen explained, things had gone full circle, and we were now ready for the next season in life and ministry. After several discussions with the leadership team or church session as they called it in Townsend Street, Kathleen and I were formally welcomed to the church one Sunday morning. We still knew many of the people there, and many were delighted to see us "back home." Well, at least most of them were!

You see, we thought everyone loved us and that everyone would welcome us back, but we were in for a shock, and we didn't have to wait too long for that shock to manifest. In fact, it manifested on the very first Sunday morning we were back. Without going into details, what we didn't foresee was that the Jackie and Kathleen who had left Townsend Street for Bible College 15 years earlier, and the Jackie and Kathleen who were now pastor and pastor's wife, would not be seen by some as the same Jackie and Kathleen who had left back in 1977. Not that it meant anything to us or to most of the people in Townsend Street, but sadly it did to a few, and sadly those few were among those we had loved and respected.

We had agreed with Pastor Eric McComb that we would give this at least three months, although we had genuinely gone intending to settle there. We had seen some very encouraging things taking place, especially with the increase in the numbers of young people, some who had previously left but returned when they knew we were there. However, it was after six very challenging months that we finally made the decision to leave. I was not running away from anything or from anyone. The only time I ever ran from a man, was when he was firing shots at me. No! I was not running; I was making a purposed conscious decision to end that chapter and to turn the page to a new season without the responsibility of church.

There were many tears from those who had welcomed us just six months earlier and who clearly wanted us to remain. However, both Kathleen and I were very much at peace and were happy to be moving on. We both knew we had tried to make it work but were disappointed that it hadn't, while I left with the added feeling that perhaps I had not heard God on this. However, I knew I could now once again focus on developing the Stadium Youth and Community Centre and that I could do so without the distraction of church. Now that sounds bad, I know, but that's how it was.

Kathleen was also happy that she could now focus again on developing Hobby Horse Playgroup without worrying about what was going on elsewhere. But I must admit, that we left wondering why we even went there in the first place. How could what looked like a mistake fit in with God's plans for our lives? It would take several years for us to find an answer, but find the answer we did.

Revelation in Israel

At that time, I was also serving as youth director for the Elim Church in Ireland, and as such I had been invited to attend a youth conference in Jerusalem. While I was there, I met two very special people. The first was Tony Campolo, a man I had the greatest respect for, before ever meeting him. I brought Kathleen a photo of Tony Campolo and me together, and told her that he had asked for a photo to be taken so he could take it back to his friends in Philadelphia, as proof he had met Jack McKee in Israel and that I was happy to oblige! Kathleen normally believed everything I told her, but I could not convince her that Tony has a photo of him and me on his fridge in Philadelphia or wherever he lives in the USA these days!

Tony Campolo was the main speaker at the conference, but the other person I met was Professor Mal Fletcher from Australia. I had also heard of Mal before this trip. In fact, I had read his book on 'Youth, the Endangered Species.' I had no idea he was there until the first conference meeting, when he led worship and introduced Tony Campolo. I made the most of this opportunity, especially spending some quality time with Mal Fletcher regarding his heart to reach the youth of the 90s generation. Having done so, I couldn't wait to get back home to share with Kathleen about the conference and about those I had met but more importantly, about how God had spoken directly to my spirit about launching a new church in Belfast. Kathleen shares about this next:

"When Jackie got home from Israel, he shared with me some of his experiences and talked much about the people he had met, but I think the most important thing he shared was how he had sat on the lawn of a hotel in Jerusalem speaking with Mal Fletcher. He told me that as he sat there speaking with Mal, he believed God spoke clearly to his heart. He did not claim it was the audible voice of God, yet he knew it was God who was speaking to him, and he was convinced that God had told him right there in Jerusalem that when he returned to Belfast, he was to start a church, but not just another church. Jackie really felt that this was his next challenge or his next call from God.

"I had seen that look on Jackie's face before, and especially since that night in 1977 when I returned home from the women's meeting at Townsend Street. That was the night he had told me that God had spoken to him about going to Bible College, and so I knew how serious he now was about starting a new church within the Shankill community. It made me realise that the idea of not being a pastor's wife would be a short-lived one and that I needed to think again about helping to pastor a church, but I understood it would not be just another church. To be honest, I had no idea what that meant at that time, but it would soon become clear.

"For the next three days, it was like Jackie was back in Israel, because I hardly saw him. He spent most of them alone in his study, thinking and writing out ideas as to what this so-called new church would look like and what it might be called. He talked over some of those ideas with me as we shared tea and coffee together, although speaking it out was more to do with him trying to think it through rather than seeking my opinion. He seemed to know where he was going with this, although he did struggle with the name. One of the names he shared with me was Hosanna Christian Fellowship. He showed me the name with cartoon drawings of musical notes and a little cartoon character that looked like him standing with his hands raised in worship, but out of the few names he had shared with me, the one he finally settled on was New Life Fellowship. And so that was it. We were now moving forward to the launch of New Life Fellowship."

Kathleen was well and truly on board, and so having prayed about this and having drunk more coffee in those few days than in weeks, I then spoke with a few people who at that time were without a church. I knew them and understood they were looking to get their spiritual teeth into a new challenge. I then put together some literature and began to advertise the start date for New Life Fellowship. But as soon as the word got out, there was an immediate reaction from one of the UVF spokespersons who put an article into the local newspaper stating, "The Shankill Doesn't Need Another Church." Ironically, it revealed an interest that both he and the UVF had in church and their uncanny insight into the Shankill's spiritual requirements.

However, we were not launching just another church! That was never our intention! Our intention was to launch a church that would touch the lives of young people who were being impacted by paramilitary groups and by drugs and criminality. So, regardless of negative comments and of clear opposition from some, New Life Fellowship was launched on 4th July 1993. The people flocked in that night. Yep! A grand total of 14 attended that first night, and five of those were Kathleen, me, and our three children (the McKee family); so, the five of us, plus nine others. What a start!

One of those who attended that first night was Margaret McCurley, who has remained by our sides from then to this day. Margaret has been a great personal friend, a rock, and very supportive at times of great personal need, along with her husband, Billy. From that first night with just a handful of people, we were off and running again as Pastor Jack and Kathleen the pastor's wife; something we seriously thought we had left behind and were not looking to go back to, but we were now once again in charge of a church, albeit with a crowd of 14, in the little upper room within Stadium Youth and Community Centre.

Some people run after the ministry, the titles, and the position, but this was never my motivation. My focus was always on serving Christ by going through whatever door He opened and by reaching out to a people who were my people, bone of my bone and flesh of my flesh. That's how I've always felt about the people of the Shankill community. So, although we said we would not pastor another church, within 18 months of leaving Ballysillan Elim, we had launched New Life Fellowship. This was not something we had purposely set out to do, but we didn't have the final word, but rather, in the words of the song, "Who has the final say? Jehovah has the final say."

I knew that night that what we were doing was ground-breaking and that the launch of New Life Fellowship would provide something that Kathleen and I both believed was missing in terms of a spiritual heart within our community outreach activities – the need for a spiritual home for ourselves and for those we were reaching within our community.

Chapter 9

Life and Death Gathers

So, we launched New Life Fellowship as a church on the Shankill Road on Sunday 4th July 1993, believing we were bringing the same old Gospel story that the church had been preaching for centuries. However, we were bringing it in a fresh way by being relevant to the generation we are called to reach while remaining authentic to the Word of God, true to the mission of the church and in keeping with the Great Commission of Christ to preach the Gospel and make disciples.

One of the things we did in the early days of New Life was to develop a church-based youth group and children's ministry. To help us achieve this, we brought in one of our pastors from England, Jim Bailey, who is also a musician and singer/songwriter, and who at that time had an amazing ministry to children and young people. The date we had chosen for this training day was Saturday 23rd October 1993, a day that would be etched into the collective mind of the Shankill community, never to be forgotten. This was not because of Jim Bailey, although that's no reflection on Jim as you'll see, and not because of our training programme; we would remember this day for a very different reason - a tragic and deathly reason.

Saturday 23rd October 1993

Given that Jim Bailey was well known among our Elim churches even here in Northern Ireland, we knew he would be an attraction to others, and so we invited youth groups and children's workers to join with us from other churches. It worked, because on that Saturday morning we had a good turnout of youth and children's workers, not only from New Life but also from other churches across Northern Ireland. After putting in a good morning of training, we stopped for lunch. But what happened next was to literally shake our world. While we were having lunch, our building was suddenly shaken by the impact of a bomb that had gone off on the Shankill Road, not far from where we were. It was one of the most notorious and ruthless terror atrocities in Northern Ireland's conflict. It has been remembered since then as 'The Shankill Bomb'.

The bomb was carried into Frizzell's Fish Shop by two IRA Bombers on a busy Saturday afternoon when the Shankill Road was filled with shoppers; men, women and children – all expendable as far as the IRA was concerned. When the dust had settled, it became clear that nine innocent people had lost their lives, and dozens more were critically injured, some with life-changing injuries. Among the dead, were young people and children. How ironic and tragic that, while we were reaching out to young people and children within our community, the IRA was killing them.

I remember how, like many others in our community, Kathleen cried throughout the day and through that night. She showed her motherly instincts and emotions, feeling for those parents who had lost children, weeping for those children killed in such a brutal way. On the other hand, I, while being deeply upset by what had happened, felt the anger and rage that many were feeling that day, staying focused on the news and wondering who was dead and what the final total would be of those killed and injured. Once again, as individuals, but also collectively as a community, we were stunned and numbed. So many had been totally traumatised, including those who were close to the bomb or had just walked past it when it exploded, but especially those families that had lost a precious loved one.

It was less than two years since our own children and our young people at church had lost their 17-year-old friend, Andrew Johnston, and now they were experiencing the loss of several within our community. Among those who died that day, was 14-year-old Leanne Murray, whose life was ended so violently by those who claim to be victims. Leanne was not just a statistic; she was someone's little daughter and sister. She was also in the same class at school as our daughter, Chara, and other young women who, by this time, were attending New Life Fellowship.

Kathleen and I went to see young Leanne Murray's mother, Gina. Kathleen writes the following: "I was broken-hearted as I entered Gina Murray's home. There was such a feeling of loss I wondered what I could possibly say. I knew that words would never be enough. It was as much as I could do just to be there and reach out to Gina as one mother to another. At the very least, she should know she was not on her own during such a time of deep sadness. Gina sat in her living room and was beyond consoling, as she tearfully held on tightly to a shoe belonging to young Leanne that had been recovered from the bomb site. It was like that shoe was all that Gina could hold on to, knowing that her little girl had been wearing it when she was brutally killed".

Leanne's brother Gary would later come into the Centre and sit with me in my office, stunned and still in shock, just looking for somewhere to sit and someone who would listen. We sat drinking coffee and chatting, Gary speaking about Leanne and how he was struggling with the loss of his little sister but also struggling with his feelings of anger. At the same time, he was concerned about his mother. I wanted to keep an open door and to create the opportunity for Gary to express how he felt, which was so important for him at that time.

Like many others across our community, Kathleen and I did our best to reach out and do what we could to help those who were hurting, which was the entire community. Regardless of who the intended target was that day, this was an attack on the whole Protestant community on the Shankill Road. More would have died had it not been for the immediate response of local people and emergency services who worked through the day and night, clearing the rubble and rescuing those who were still alive.

The media was all over the place, and so, like other local church ministers and community leaders who were on the ground that day doing what they could to help, I was interviewed on camera to express how the community and I felt about the bombing. During the interview, I totally and rightly condemned the IRA for the bombing and killing of innocent Shankill Road shoppers. But I also hit out against the UDA and the UFF. Their activities at that time were used by the IRA as a pathetic attempt to justify the massacre of nine innocent people and the injuries inflicted on many others. As a result of my outspoken remarks against the UDA, the leadership of that organisation misunderstood something I had said and took great offence. That led to them literally sentencing me to death. This organisation was never slow in taking life, whether Catholic or Protestant - even some within our own community, including young Shankill Road men that we had personally worked with in our Centre.

I was quickly made aware of the death sentence! However, I did not tell Kathleen about it. When it came to situations like this, and there were many, I did not share details with her. However, I did at times let her know I was going to meet certain people and when she should expect me home. One particular Monday night, not long after the Shankill Bomb, I left home to meet with some people at church. I let Kathleen know where I was going and told her I'd be home by around 9.30pm. Kathleen picks up the story of that night from here:

"Jackie told me he was going to meet with the Evangelism Team at church and that he'd be home around 9.30pm. But he also told me in no uncertain terms to keep the door locked and not to open it to anyone unless I knew who they were. He spoke in a way that made me suspicious and concerned that something was wrong, but I had no idea what it was. The night was quiet. There was nothing out of the ordinary and nothing to be concerned about, but I had no idea that someone was outside our home, hiding in the darkness.

"9.30pm came and went, and Jackie was not home. 10pm came and went, and Jackie was still not home. I remember going to the window and pulling back the blinds to look for Jackie's car. I looked down through the darkness of our street, wondering where he was. The street was dark and quiet, with not a moving vehicle in sight. We had very few neighbours at that time. There were only a few homes on our site, as we were still on a building site with several uncompleted homes right next to ours.

"That night I felt isolated and didn't quite know what to do. As the night went on, I became more concerned. I could now hear the clock ticking the seconds and the minutes away. At 10.30pm, Jackie still wasn't home. It was now more than three hours since he had left, and my concern levels were now quite high. Finally, as I was thinking over my options, wondering what I should do and who I should phone, I heard a car pull into the driveway. To my relief, it was Jackie. It was 10.40pm, but I was so glad when he turned his key in the door and finally came into the house.

"While Jackie was taking his jacket and shoes off and doing his best to explain why he was late home, I went into the kitchen to make tea. As I did so, someone came knocking on the door. Jackie and I both froze as we looked at each other. He put his finger to his mouth, motioning to me to be quiet. After a few moments, he looked out the window and could see someone standing at our front door. It was one of our closest neighbours from across the street. Jackie opened the door and brought him in, but we had no idea why he came knocking at that time of the night.

"He told Jackie that he wasn't sure if this meant anything to him, but he said that two men had been watching our house from around 7.30pm that night and that they had only just left at 10.30pm. This meant that they had been outside our home for three hours, from ten minutes after Jackie had left the house at 7.20pm, until ten minutes before he arrived home. It also meant that I had no idea that there were two armed men outside my home that night and that they were there for three hours, waiting to murder my husband when he returned home. I knew I had reason to be concerned, but I had no idea how serious it was."

Kathleen and I didn't sleep well that night. In fact, I didn't go to bed until well after midnight, often checking outside, making sure that whoever it was outside our home that night had not doubled back. Within a short period of time, I had it confirmed, through two different sources, that the two gunmen outside our home were two brothers, 19 and 21-year-olds. They were part of the UDA leadership team that had passed the death sentence unanimously.

We also learned that these two young men were part of the UDA's C Company based in the Denmark Street and Lower Shankill area, the very street we were married from, and where we returned to for a few years before leaving for Bible College. It was where the IRA had tried to murder me and my friend Michael, where Michael was finally shot dead in his home, the street where I had walked behind the coffins of several friends, who the IRA or the INLA had murdered. Yet, it was from this very street and the surrounding Lower Shankill area where the UDA leadership sentenced me to death.

Kathleen explains further from her perspective: "Of all the places to pass a death sentence on Jackie! The Lower Shankill was our home community. My family was the first to move into Denmark Street. I left No.2 in a wedding car, while Jackie left No.5 to meet me at the church altar. With others in Denmark Street, we went through the grief of losing friends and neighbours murdered by the IRA. Jackie avoided two attempts on his life when we lived at No.9 for four years. Jackie was a member of the UDR the whole time we lived there. This was the same area that my friend Elizabeth and I had led many little children by the hands through the streets to Sunshine Corner in Townsend Street Elim. It was where both of our parents and families still lived, and yet it was from that same area within the Lower Shankill that this death threat came. I was shocked and heartbroken but thankful that God had intervened. Let me explain how He did.

"After our neighbour had left our home that night, Jackie explained to me that the meeting with the Evangelism Team had gone on to around 10pm. Jackie was about to leave the church at 10.10pm when Roger Abrol, leader of the Evangelism Team, told him and the team that he sensed danger for Jackie, but he had no idea why. Roger, nor any of the team members knew what was going on. They knew nothing of any death threat. So, when Roger said he sensed danger and offered to pray, Jackie readily accepted the offer.

"So, they prayed with Jackie, and they did so for twenty minutes, not knowing that as they were praying, two gunmen were outside our home waiting on Jackie. Yet, it was as they were praying that the two gunmen gave up waiting! They had been there for three hours, yet they left our street while Roger and the team were praying! We both felt deeply that night that God had intervened; otherwise, Jackie would not have survived. It was tough trying to sleep that night, but we did so, knowing that the God we served neither slumbers nor sleeps and that we are surrounded by a host of angels so that there were more for us than those who were against us."

The following morning Kathleen was back at Hobby Horse Playgroup, and I was back at the Centre. However, within just two days from that Monday night, the two brothers were arrested. They were driving along the Shankill Road in the direction of the Centre when the police stopped them. They were carrying loaded weapons in the car and were eventually sentenced to seven years in prison for arms and explosive offences. The death sentence was never carried out, and although we don't know the full reason why, yet we're thankful for the twenty minutes of prayer that literally saved my life that night and saved Kathleen from the horror of seeing her husband gunned down on our doorstep.

Pushing fear to one side

I know the Bible says, *"God has not given us a spirit of fear,"*[3] but there are times when it is not so easy to be fearless! Like so many others, we had already gone through so much as husband and wife, and as a family. Whether it was the accidental firing of a gun during our first year of marriage that almost killed Kathleen, the attempted bombing of the car, the loss of close friends and neighbours, or the loss of young Andrew Johnston. Whether it was being part of a community that had been impacted by several bombings that had taken the lives of quite a number of innocent people of all ages, including children, and had severely maimed many more. Yes, there are things we all learn to live with, but then there are those moments that are much more difficult to come to terms with when even the strongest among us experience a real sense of fear.

Kathleen and I had no idea when we left Ballysillan Elim that the next number of years would present greater challenges, and certainly not the kind of challenges that Bible College could have prepared us for. Instead, these would be challenges that we would go through together as husband and wife, for better or for worse, yet we did so knowing with confidence that God's hand was upon us for our good.

Kathleen says, "Yes, there were times when I was fearful; yet no matter what came against us, I knew I had to keep moving forward and that I had to stay focused on being a mother to three children, and I needed to stay focused on being the Senior Manager of Hobby Horse Playgroup.

3 2 Timothy 1:7

But to do this, I also knew that I had to push fear to one side. There was no room for fear. So, beyond the Shankill Bomb and the attempt on Jackie's life, I continued to develop Hobby Horse within Stadium Youth & Community Centre.

"The building was old and required many repairs and the space allocated to us could not accommodate any more than 16 children, and so we were restricted in terms of space and growth. But in 1998, Jackie told me that the Centre had plans for major redevelopment, which would help Hobby Horse grow its capacity to 24 children. We were delighted and excited by this, but then it later changed from refurbishment to plans for a completely new building that would include a purpose-built Playgroup. We were beside ourselves because that meant we would not only be able to increase our numbers, but it also meant having our own outside play area for the children, something we had not had from when we started in September 1989. However, we were told the new building would take up to two years to complete, so we agreed that we would move into temporary accommodation. We were happy to do so, as we were excited about the new building and the new purpose-built Playgroup."

Kathleen and her team were now looking forward to seeing how things would develop, but the first thing we needed to do was to find temporary accommodation. So the old Stadium was sold to the Shankill Partnership, a community organisation that I'd helped to establish when I was on the board of the Greater Shankill Development Agency. The deal was done with the support of Making Belfast Work, a government funding body that was putting up around £3M for a new Youth and Community building on the site of the old Stadium. The Partnership agreed to purchase the building and the site for £120,000, but it was also agreed that Stadium Projects and Hobby Horse would return as core tenants.

A local builder saw a great opportunity for building housing on the site, so he offered £240,000 to purchase the old Stadium. But I never even brought the offer to the Stadium management team as I wanted to keep the site firmly in the hands of the community and was happy for Stadium projects and Hobby Horse to be a part of the future of the proposed new building. Unknown to me, however, although not surprisingly, other influences were at work behind the scenes.

Over several months, I met with architects to discuss all the requirements for the new building, including Hobby Horse and its new outside play area. I remember Kathleen's excitement when she was able to discuss with them the needs of Hobby Horse. Like me, she had great hopes for the future but had no idea that no matter how often we would meet with the architects, designers and suppliers, we would never see the inside of the new building. Kathleen would never see the inside of her new purpose-built playgroup, and the children of Hobby Horse would never get to use the outside play area built specifically for them.

The first sign that something was seriously wrong, was when someone told me that they had been in a meeting where a well-known person on the Shankill Road had said, "When we get Jack McKee out, he's not getting back in." But it wasn't just about Jack McKee; it was about those who the Centre employed, and about the young people who were benefitting from our programmes and activities, and also about the children and staff in Hobby Horse. So how did this affect Hobby Horse? Kathleen shares the following:

"All of our staff members were totally shocked and extremely disappointed when they were told that they would not be moving into the new building. In fact, the truth is, we were all angry, but we determined that we would not let it get to us. Stadium Projects moved into a building purchased with the money from the sale of the old Stadium, but the building was upstairs above several shops on the Shankill Road and was therefore not suitable for our playgroup. But New Life had been given another building. It was the Townsend Street Elim Church, that had sadly closed its doors.

"New Life moved into the church building in Townsend Street. What helped us was that the building was on the ground-floor level and was able to accommodate Hobby Horse. It was perfect. Even though we never did get to move back into the new Centre that was built on the old Stadium site, the fact is we were happy where we were in Townsend Street, although that also would not last, because being with Jackie meant things kept changing and developing."

Chapter 10
From a Box Office to Church

We started off in the old Stadium Cinema on the Shankill Road in September 1989 with indoor football, snooker, the Mile Café, and other activities. Kathleen started Hobby Horse Playgroup in a little back room. After ten years in the Old Stadium - challenging but good years - we moved to two other locations. One was the building above shops on the Shankill Road that belonged to the Church of God, Boys' Brigade, that we purchased and called Top House. The other was the Elim Church in Townsend Street, where Kathleen and I attended for three months, as described earlier in this book.

Several years after our six-month "stint" at Townsend Street, the Elim Church sadly closed its doors. The few people who had remained to the very end, finally moved to other churches. Afterwards, the building remained empty for some time until, and without any effort or enquiries on my part, we were asked if we could use the building. This led to it being 'given' to us to use for New Life Fellowship, but we were also able to facilitate Hobby Horse Playgroup.

We were in Townsend Street for six years, and during that time, some of our family members and neighbours from the Lower Shankill and Denmark Street area came to the church and committed their lives to Christ. These included my own mum, known as Maggie McKee, Kathleen's sister Sally, whose son Robert was the one killed in the motorbike accident in 1978 while we were in France, Sammy Miller's wife Violet, mentioned earlier as one of those whom Kathleen regularly sat next to in church, whose brother Bobby had been murdered, and whose husband Sammy had been shot and left paralysed. Then there was also Violet's daughter, Tracey, who later married Craig Seawright, son of Democratic Unionist Councillor, George Seawright, who was sadly shot dead by the IRA.

And so, while leaving the 'Old Stadium' was painful, and while not getting back into the new building was frustrating, it was not the end of the road for us, but rather the end of one season and the beginning of another. We had church in Top House for a while, and man, did we have church! Then we moved to Townsend Street. That proved to be the right move for the church at that time and was also a good move for Hobby Horse Playgroup as we were able to locate the playgroup in what was formerly a Youth Hall located next to the church, something for which Kathleen and her team were truly grateful. Kathleen writes the following:

"The Youth Hall was ideal for us as a playgroup. This became our own dedicated space where we could set everything out and leave it without having to put it all away at the end of each day. However, after about a year, the feud broke out between the UVF and the UDA (mentioned in Chapter 7). That was when the need arose for families to have somewhere to store their furniture. It was then that we made the decision to move the playgroup into the main church building for several months, while we used the playgroup to store furniture.

"My staff members were amazing. No matter what I asked them to do, they stepped up every time to every demand and challenge. My two main staff members, who have also become good friends, are Maureen and Lorraine. They have been with me for many years and are now the two most senior and most important key workers within the project. Maureen has been our Playgroup Manager now for several years, and Lorraine, our Senior Supervisor. They're a great team, and I love and appreciate them both. They have been alongside me in every move, during the good times and the not so good."

No let-up from the threats

Moving from the old Stadium to Top House and to the church in Townsend Street might have changed our location, but it didn't change things in terms of negative attitudes from others, or our determination to keep going. Kathleen writes:

"Jackie always felt the need to keep speaking out against terrorism, drug dealing and other forms of criminality. It was hard for him not to do so as he had good reason. We had lost Davy Douglas to the UVF and Andrew Johnston to the IPLO while reaching out to the community from the "Old Stadium." And while reaching out from Top House and Townsend Street, we lost other young men who were murdered by both the UVF and the UDA. Some of these were young men who had been in our home, for whom I had personally made tea. But it wasn't enough for Jackie to stand on the platform on Sundays and just preach sermons while these things were happening during the week. Moreover, it wasn't just the Shankill because the same thing was happening to young men across the wall in the Falls community, who were being beaten, shot and murdered by the IRA and others.

"Jackie decided to write a book that would reflect some of these stories. It was called 'Through Terror and Adversity' and was released in 2002. I remember one day when our phone rang at home. I heard Jackie speak with the person on the other end and knew that there was something wrong. I could hear him say he would not be meeting anyone that day, as he had other things to do that were more important and that he would not be cancelling anything to go anywhere. I could hear him say that he would meet with the person on Friday, but by the reaction, it was clear that his response didn't go down well. Friday was two days away.

"When Jackie came off the phone, he saw that I was concerned, and while he didn't always tell me everything that was going on, he did feel the need to tell me about this phone call. He told me who it was, and that the person wanted to meet him down at the Eagle. I don't know too much about the Eagle, but I did know that it was the HQ for the UVF on the Shankill Road. For ten minutes Jackie tried to get on with doing other things, but it was clear he was concerned about the call he had just received, as was I. He finally told me that he was going to call back and agree to meet the person that day in the Eagle. He had no idea what the issue was, but knew there was one, and so he decided it would be best for him to know sooner rather than later.

"So, Jackie made the call back and told the person that he would be there in fifteen minutes. He then told me where he was going and who he was going to meet. He then said that if he did not call me back within an hour, I was to phone the police and let them know where he was. And then off he went. So, I waited and prayed, which is something I'd done often over the years. I prayed for Jackie's protection, that everything would be okay and that I would hear from him soon. The minutes seemed like hours, but thankfully I didn't have to wait out the complete hour, and thankfully I didn't have to make that call to the police.

"It was just around 30 minutes that had passed when the phone rang. I lifted it, hoping it was Jackie, and it was. He told me the meeting only lasted about five minutes and that he was back in the car and on his way home. When he arrived, I was quite emotional and gave him such a hug. He explained what happened; when he got to the Eagle, he was able to park the car right outside on the main road. Before he went inside, he walked around the car so that people would recognise him and see him going inside.

"He continued to explain that the person he was speaking to on the phone had been waiting for him with some other men, two of whom were known to him. He was invited into the back room of the Eagle by the person he had spoken to on the phone. Only the two of them went inside the room. The door was closed behind them, and there on the table was a copy of Jackie's book, *'Through Terror and Adversity'*. The person challenged him regarding one of the stories in the book relating to a death threat from the UVF. According to Jackie's account in the book, it was relayed to him by one of the Brigade Staff members of the UVF. The person Jackie was speaking to was the very person he had written about, although he hadn't named him.

"Jackie was informed that all Brigade Staff members denied it was them, and they wanted to know who it was, which is why some were sitting outside. This put Jackie in an awkward and dangerous situation. He told me that he looked at the person across the table and said to him, "There are three who know the truth about that story and who know who that person was. I know who it was. The person who passed on the death threat knows who it was, and God knows who it was, and I'm happy to leave it at that." Jackie said that at that point, the person came around the table and shook his hand because it seems that's all he wanted to hear. The door was opened, and within moments, he was walking past the men who were still sitting outside. Soon he was home, and all was well.

"However, to be honest, this really did get to Jackie. It shook him, like someone falling off a motorbike, but he knew he had to get back onto the bike, and so not long after this I remember Jackie saying to me that he was going to carry a 7ft wooden cross around the Dividing Wall between the Shankill and the Falls, and was going to do so for 40 days. He felt he needed to lift the Cross above the gun as a symbol of peace. My response was, "As long as you don't ask me to do it with you," which he didn't. But he did do the walk for 40 days. He thought this would be a one-off event but had no idea it would lead to many similar Cross walks since then, many of which I did join in. But so too did many others from New Life and from other churches, including people from across the world as far away as Alaska and New Zealand, including Arthur Blessitt from Colorado."

Home is attacked, but worse was to come

As a pastor, I've always tried to be protective of the church, and the same applies to our home and to Kathleen. I never wanted to attract danger to anyone. I didn't even want it for me, but my main concern was always for others. Even my own brothers would say to me at times, "You be careful that you don't bring any trouble to this family," and I was. But it didn't always work.

In 2005 we were still in Townsend Street and Top House, getting on with church and with Hobby Horse Playgroup and other programmes. All seemed to be well until one day, two of the men in New Life had their taxis attacked. Windows were smashed on both, and one was set on fire and completely destroyed. As their pastor, I called to see the two men. During our conversation it was suggested that the church should think about setting up its own Christian Taxi Company. Well, within just a few weeks, we launched Liberty Taxis. Several drivers signed up, and people were keen to call us. However, there was a problem! The local paramilitaries were far from happy as they had a vested interest in existing taxi companies and were losing drivers and customers to Liberty Taxis.

Within the first few weeks, it was doing amazingly well, so much so, that it was causing concern in the ranks of other taxi companies and other organisations. One of our taxis was attacked and damaged with a concrete slab. Other drivers were being challenged by local paramilitaries and by other taxi drivers. Telephone wires going into the church for Liberty Taxis were cut, but worse was to come. Our home was attacked in the middle of the night at 3.30am, while Kathleen and I were sleeping. Our car was petrol- bombed and engulfed in flames in our driveway, and every window at the front of our home was smashed. Although the attackers did not get inside, they left such a mess, causing thousands of pounds worth of damage. My heart went out to Kathleen that night as I watched her look with shock around her home.

Car bombed & Home attacked at 3.30am

Kathleen shares how she felt that night:

"I stood looking at our home and the mess that had been created. This was my home, our family home, a home that was open to everyone, where we'd entertained many and where some stayed as a safe place. Yet here it was with windows smashed, walls covered in paint, and our car nothing more than a blackened empty shell. All I could do was to stand in the middle of the mess and cry. My home was okay when we went to bed that night, but it was not now.

"Looking back, I realise that this was not something that Bible College had prepared me for, the fact is, this should never happen to any woman or any home.

"Within a few days of the attack, the police came back to our home. This time it was to inform Jackie that Police Intelligence had received information from a police informant, that at least one of the Liberty Taxi drivers was to be shot dead within 24 hours and that Jackie would also be targeted. The Police Officer asked Jackie to sign a piece of paper confirming he had been made aware of the threat, and within moments he was gone. It was not just about taxis, a car and a home. This was now about life and death.

"Not willing to have the death of any of the drivers on his conscience, Jackie, within hours, brought the drivers of Liberty Taxis together and explained what had been happening and then told them it was time to call it a day and bring Liberty Taxis to an end. There was a mixed reaction from the drivers and people across the community to the attack on our home and against the death threats. Even some of the members of paramilitary groups were against what had happened, but most were afraid to say anything. However, not everyone was afraid to speak up.

"One person, the father of a boy who attended Hobby Horse Playgroup but who was also a member of a paramilitary group, took it upon himself to go into the headquarters of the organisation and complain about the attack on our home. Although he was a member of that organisation, he had also attended New Life at times, and played on the church's football team, New Life Young Men's. We knew him quite well but didn't know he had spoken against the attack on our home until several weeks later when we were told what he'd done. But we were also told he was badly beaten and ended up in hospital for having done so. Jackie met with him and thanked him."

Although I tried, it was not possible to shield Kathleen from everything that was going on, especially when it affected the young people we were working with through the church or our community programmes; like those who would frequent our home for after-church games like Balderdash, Monopoly and Mafia, or for barbeques. Most of the young people who came to New Life back in the early days were not caught up in drugs or paramilitaries. But as time went on, we connected with young people from across the wider community and began to see more and more come to the church from very challenging backgrounds.

During our time in Townsend Street, prior to our home being attacked, a young man called Jameson Lockhart started to attend New Life with his older brother Joe. Joe had already committed his life to Christ but was still facing his own major challenges. He was delighted to see Jameson attending New Life and was even more delighted the night that Jameson committed his life to Christ, and he was happy that Jameson made New Life his spiritual home.

However, not long after our home had been attacked in May 2005, Jameson told me he had handed £40,000 in cash over to a UVF Commander on the Shankill Road for personal protection; and the protection of heavy equipment he owned and used at work. A few weeks later, I told Kathleen I was going to Jameson's house and that I might not be home until the early hours of the morning. It was another one of those moments when I left Kathleen with just enough information to know that something serious was happening and that Jameson was in danger.

Kathleen explains: "When Jackie told me he was going to Jameson's, I knew right away that something was wrong. I didn't often question things, I just trusted that Jackie knew what he was doing and that God would keep him safe, but at that time, I did express my concern. Jackie explained that Jameson had been told that the UVF were planning to kill him and that he was going to sit with him for a while, but that all would be well. Once again, I was left wondering but also hoping and praying that everything would be okay. It was after midnight when Jackie finally came home. Nothing had happened, and all was well, at least for that night.

"It was a few weeks later on the 1ˢᵗ July when Jackie had planned to walk along the Shankill Road while carrying the same 7ft Cross he had carried previously for 40 days. It was something he had now done several times around the Shankill and Falls, but this time it was just the Shankill and just for that one day. There was a reason that Jackie chose the 1ˢᵗ July. That's the date the UVF march along the Shankill Road every year. He always believed that they, in partnership with the UDA, were involved in attacking our home back in May, and he wanted to make the point that the Cross is mightier than the gun by lifting the Cross above the gun. That was one of those times when I, along with others from New Life and including several visitors from a church in Virginia, USA, had planned to walk along the footpath as Jackie walked along the centre of the road on his own with the Cross.

"But just before we left the church to do the walk, one of our women, Mary Warden, leaned over Jackie's shoulder and whispered to him, "Jameson Lockhart has just been shot dead." Jameson had been gunned down by the UVF just thirty minutes earlier inside his truck in East Belfast. He became another young man that we at New Life had to bury; a young man I had made tea for and another young man murdered by a paramilitary group within our own community. I remember going with Jackie to see Jameson's mother at her home. I remember once again holding and embracing another broken-hearted mother on the Shankill Road who had lost a child, only this time it was to paramilitaries in the Shankill community.

"Adding to her pain was the fact that her 17-year-old daughter, Denise, had previously died while taking drugs, that apparently she had got from members of the UDA in the Lower Shankill. This made me even more aware of the importance of our work, not only within New Life but also Hobby Horse. Many of the children attending the playgroup were coming from communities and possibly homes, that were being affected by these kinds of violent activities."

Chapter 11

Not Another Move!

"Not another move!" was Kathleen's exasperated comment. Hobby Horse had settled quite well within its new home in Townsend Street, but in 2006, New Life had decided to sell the church building and buy a warehouse about a mile away in a different part of the Shankill community. Kathleen explains what lay behind her "Not another move" outburst:

"We loved where we were. We had been back in the Youth Hall for several years. It had been painted and decorated and refurbished by John Legge, who was at that time one of the pastors at New Life, but who had also been a joiner by trade and had done lots of work for Jackie in the old Stadium and for New Life in its new home in Townsend Street. John transformed the Youth Hall to make it look like a proper playgroup area. It was looking great. Everyone was happy there, so when Jackie told me that the church was being sold and they were buying a warehouse, I remember frustratingly saying, "What? Not another move!"

"My next question was, "Where would we go?" Unfortunately, the warehouse would not be ready for many months, perhaps much longer. We had no idea! However, thankfully the Presbyterians came to our rescue. The local Presbyterian Church was based just yards from where we were in Townsend Street and it had a Youth Hall, that at that time was vacant. This hall was ideal for our purposes and thankfully was made available to us. So, we made the move to the Presbyterian Church in April 2006 but had no idea that this would be our home for the next five years! Yep! Five years!

"Although the Presbyterian Church was amazing, and we were made to feel at home, we always felt like we were living in someone else's home. This was the first time since we started in 1989 that we'd been separated from Stadium Projects. We were never used to being on our own, but we always had others around us, even though they were in different parts of the building. At least we knew there was always someone else in the building, whereas in the Presbyterian Church, we seldom saw anyone from one day to the next. We were also used to just walking into Hobby Horse early in the mornings without having to think about heating, especially during the winter, but in our new location, we were responsible for opening up the building in the mornings and locking it at the end of each day. We were also responsible for putting the heating on and off. We'd obviously been spoiled by New Life and Stadium Projects!

"During the winter months, I would leave home around 6.30am to ensure the heating was on and that the room was warm enough for the children, who would arrive at around 9am. Another drawback, was that the Boys' Brigade used the room every Saturday night, which meant we had to put everything away on Friday afternoons and then put it all back out again on Monday mornings before the children arrived. Jackie would get out of bed every Monday morning and go with me to the playgroup to help me put out all the tables, chairs, toys, sandpit, and all the other play equipment so that everything would be ready for the children arriving at 9am. Lorraine Barr would arrive shortly after 8am and help us finish off. There would be time enough for a cup of tea and a chat after Jackie left and before everyone else started to arrive.

"It's hard to believe it was five years, but it was five amazing years, with close to 150 pre-school children being in our care during that time.

But we always felt isolated and missed the company of the staff and volunteers at Stadium Projects. They made the transition in 2009 to the new location at the warehouse in Northumberland Street. It had been partly refurbished by October 2009 and was open to the public as City Life Centre, accommodating New Life and several community offices.

"By January 2011, a coffee shop had been opened to the public within City Life Centre. Other areas of the building had also been refurbished, but more importantly for Hobby Horse, was the fact that we were finally able to move to City Life Centre. So, it was in January 2011; we finally moved into an area within the Centre that was dedicated solely for the use of Hobby Horse Playgroup and for our after-school Butterfly Club. It really felt like we were home, and we were, and still are to this day.

City Life Centre – Hobby Horse Playgroup and New Life City Church

Finances where?

"Helping to run a church is one thing but looking after a pre-school playgroup, besides running an after-school project for children with additional needs, is something entirely different. It's always been my heart to work with children, going back to my days in Brown Square and Denmark Street. It was always rewarding to know that you were helping in the early development of children and being a support to their families, but it's never easy, especially concerning finances. Having children in our care from the Shankill community brought its own problems because children were often coming from families with issues that were varied and were often a reflection of inner-city life in Belfast.

"For example, many of our target families were on a low income or were unemployed. So our charges have always been extremely low with a nominal daily fee for the morning Playgroup, while the after-school Butterfly Club is free. The only way we can do this is due to the support we have received from Early Years and from the Department for Communities, which is mainly for the morning Playgroup, and support from Social Services for the afternoon Butterfly Club.

"However, the above support does not provide for all of our needs, which is why we place a small charge on the morning Playgroup. Even then, we still need to make applications for additional funding, besides doing our own fundraising activities involving the parents. But it's always a battle, and at times that battle was made more difficult even by those who should have known better. For example, the Northern Ireland Housing Executive took £175,000 from the overall project when the church sold its building in Townsend Street. Before the end of that financial year, the Housing Executive returned over £1M of unspent funds to central government. Think of what that could have done in our overall project!

"Then for several years, we worked in collaboration with the Riddell Nursery in the Lower Shankill. In 2015, the Riddell had gotten into some financial difficulties, which would lead to it closing its doors after having provided a service to the community over many years. We at Hobby Horse lobbied to try and save the Riddell, but we were unsuccessful. To add to the problem, because of our collaboration with the Riddell which included us having to take the lead role for funding purposes, when the Riddell finally closed its doors, we at Hobby Horse had to carry the loss of £7,000 that we had made as an advance payment. We fought for that also but lost.

"I mention this to pay tribute to the Riddell Nursery for its years of service within the Shankill Community. I do so because no one else will and because I fully understand the difficulties involved in running a childcare project within a disadvantaged community such as ours. I also want to express my disappointment that the Riddell was forced to close its doors without any serious support from any other organisation within our community.

Everybody needs somebody

"Jackie would often say, "No man is an island" (although I think he got that from someone else), but he also said, "No church is an island." I believe he was making the point that we all need someone, and that we all must be accountable to someone. This is also true of community projects, and is certainly true of Hobby Horse Playgroup. We could never have made it on our own and could never have achieved our success without the help and support of others. This included Stadium Projects, New Life City Church, the Department for Communities (formerly BRO, MBW and BAT), Early Years (formerly NIPPA), Social Services, other funding organisations, and amazing staff and volunteers. Likewise, we had an amazing management board chaired by the very capable Mrs Lesley Hance, not forgetting the many parents who faithfully brought their children to Hobby Horse throughout the years.

"I am also extremely thankful for an amazing family that's been so supportive all this time, not only to me personally but also to the work to which we know God has called us. I could have chosen an easier life (I think), but being a pastor's wife and working with many families within our community has not only been challenging and sometimes very demanding, but has been so rewarding. Having your family by your side as part of that journey has been the most rewarding of all.

"To say that I am proud of my three children would be an understatement, but each of them has honoured us as their parents. As their mother, I am delighted to have had them walking alongside us in this amazing journey. Jonathan travelled back and forth to Bible College when he was a child, and is now committed to New Life City Church and to City Life Projects. As a lead pastor within the church he stands shoulder to shoulder with Jackie. He is also the senior manager within City Life Projects, having recently taken over from Tommy Latimer who has been an amazing support for many years. Chara has also walked alongside us, living her dream in helping others live their dreams through GLOW – Giving Life Opportunities to Women. She pioneered and launched this project to help women of all ages from all communities and backgrounds. Finally, Paula has been with us as an amazing administrator in Hobby Horse Family Project, keeping everything in order and being an incredible support to me personally, especially in recent years: not least, helping to make dinner for all of us, on most Sundays.

"Our three children have now given us seven grandchildren, Judah and Eli (Jonathan's), Jackson and Cassia (Chara's), and Luke, Ethan and Ellie (Paula's). Like every child and every person, they are all unique and all very lovable. Judah is the serious one, Eli the fearless one, Jackson the sporty one, and although most of the boys are into football, Jackson is much more committed to it. Cassia is a very typical young woman who loves to clown around at other people's expense. Luke, the oldest grandchild, is big into singing and music and is the lead singer for a band called 'Casual Riots' although I'm not sure why! Ethan is also a fearless one and a risk-taker, while Ellie, our youngest grandchild, is a chatterbox just like her mum was, but is friendly with everyone and loved by all.

"Ellie is often referred to as our "miracle baby." When Paula was pregnant with Ellie, there were complications. The child was diagnosed with possible Down syndrome and other complications. It was said that she had little chance of surviving much beyond birth. Paula was offered termination, but she and William made the decision not to terminate but to give her the chance of life. When Ellie was born, there were serious complications with her heart, but all of those complications have now been resolved and no longer present any threat to her as they once did.

"However, Ellie was born with Noonan's syndrome. Regardless of that, even though it has its drawbacks, she is doing extremely well and is now attending mainstream primary school. Both Paula and William have been amazing parents, while Ellie, on the other hand, has been an amazing daughter and granddaughter. We are so thankful that they made the decision to give life, otherwise, we never would have known

this precious little girl, who for years was known to many who prayed for her across the world as Baby Ellie, but of course, she's no longer the baby that she was.

Kathleen with baby Ellie in hospital

"I am therefore so thankful for a great family and for great friends who have walked with us and allowed us to walk with them. Even as I have looked to my left and right for many years on Sunday mornings, I have felt so blessed that sitting close by have been my two amazing sisters, Sally and Marie, and blessed that sitting alongside us has been our good friends Violet Millar and Margaret McCurley. Yes, everybody needs somebody, and I'm so glad to be surrounded by many amazing somebodies."

Chapter 12

From the Square to the Palace

Many of you who will be reading this book can recall the Sunday School prize giving. Kathleen and I attended Sunday School at the Elim Church in Brown Square, we always looked forward to Presentation Day, when we'd get a Bible or a framed picture with a Bible verse on it for good attendance or for answering questions. It always marked a moment of achievement and meant so much to us. Both of us remember getting a Bible for attendance when we were young. They had a label with our names written on them and were dated by our Sunday School Teacher. We treasured these, but we had no idea that we would be receiving other kinds of presentations and awards for service and achievements within the wider community later in life.

The following awards relate to the overall work of Stadium Projects, now City Life Projects and including New Life City Church. The first ever, was the Allied Irish Bank (AIB) Better Ireland Award, an award for a Personal Development Programme called Higher Force Challenge that helped at-risk and disadvantaged young people from across our divided communities of North and West Belfast. The second, was an award for our community outreach to both Protestant and Catholic communities in Belfast presented to me and members of our team by the Prime Minister of Ireland, Bertie Ahern, in Cork. The third, was a day out to the residence of the then US Ambassador to Ireland, Jean Kennedy Smith (sister of JFK), who honoured us for our work by hosting a group of young men from Belfast at her residence in Dublin. She served us burgers and chips (fries) on huge white plates with the US Seal engraved on them, followed by vanilla and chocolate ice cream, some of which ended up on the white rug in the main living room. It was an amazing day that led to the project receiving a cheque from Liam Neeson for $18,000 when the Ambassador shared directly with him about our work with young people in Belfast.

The fourth award was an invitation to travel to Jerusalem along with the then Bob Gibson, Senior Governor of Prisons in Northern Ireland, where we were being honoured for our Higher Force Challenge programmes at a conference on crime prevention and the prevention of recidivism. We were given the opportunity to present our project to several Rabbis and Imams. The fifth was an award presented to New Life City Church at Holy Cross Chapel in Ardoyne for our peace and reconciliation work. Kathleen and I, attended the ceremony in Holy Cross and received the award, presented by Mrs Stella Empey, wife of Sir Reg Empey, former leader of the Ulster Unionist Party.

We had no idea when we left Bible College that we would ever be involved in this kind of outreach and that we'd be receiving these kinds of awards and acknowledgements, not only from those mentioned above, but also including the British Prime Minister John Major, Prince Charles and Camilla, and several other senior Government Ministers and Representatives, especially Lady Jean Mayhew who loved our work, and included visits to the White House, the US State Department, and the Senate Building in Washington DC. However, there was a sixth award that would take Kathleen, our family and me, all the way from our meagre past in Brown Square to the lavish corridors of Buckingham Palace, as explained by Kathleen:

An invitation that brought tears

"It was a day in May 2017, when an envelope dropped through the door with Jackie's name on it. He stood while he opened it, but then sat down at the dining table. I noticed him beginning to sniff and wipe his eyes like he was getting teary. I had no idea what it was, but I went over and put my arm around him as I asked, "What is it, Jackie?" He struggled to tell me, but I could finally make out that he was saying, "I've been awarded an MBE" (Member of the Order of the British Empire). Jackie had been named that year in the Queen's Birthday Honours list for outstanding service to the community. All I could hear him say was, "Why me? I don't deserve this," and then he said "No, this is not for me, this is for you, and for our family, and for everyone in New Life and everyone at City Life Centre".

"Jackie had received a letter from the Queen inviting him and me and two other family members to Buckingham Palace to receive the award. But there were two problems! The first was that we had to keep this quiet and confidential until the media formally released it. The second was that the invitation to the Palace specifically stated it was for Jackie, me, and two others. So, who were we going to leave out? Jackie wrote to the Palace, and thankfully, they permitted an additional person, which meant we would be able to bring all three of our adult children with us. This would be the first time in years that all five of us went somewhere together alone. The last time was Disney World in Florida when they were kids, but now, it would be Buckingham Palace in London.

"It was February 2018, when the five of us travelled as a family. That experience was every bit as special as actually going to the Palace. We flew to London together, got lost in the London Underground together (several times), stayed in the same hotel (not together), and dined in London together. Jackie and Jonathan got to go to Wembley Stadium to see Spurs play and beat Manchester United, which made them both very happy, while Chara, Paula and I walked around the shops. Then came the day for the Palace. We had no idea if we would actually meet the Queen or who else it might be, but this was a very special day, regardless.

"We arranged to be taken to the Palace by taxi and were dropped off at the front gate where many tourists had already gathered and where security was quite apparent. The moment we entered through the front gates and went inside, everything went like clockwork. We were immediately told what to do and where to go. Jackie was soon ushered along a hallway while we were directed into a large room where others had been gathering. It was around an hour later when the Award Ceremony began, with Prince Charles representing the Queen. One by one, those receiving awards had their names called and would enter the room.

"When the time came and we heard Jackie's name called out, I felt such a sense of righteous pride and deep appreciation for all that God had brought us through from we first met in Brown Square and our first date in the local chip shop, and now here we were, inside Buckingham Palace, being honoured for those years of service to our community. Even though Jackie stood alone, looking into the eyes of Prince Charles, we all felt we were standing right there alongside him, which is something he often acknowledged and did so with the following article that appeared in magazines and newspapers."

I know it's the done thing for those who are honoured in receiving such an award to make sure they give credit to those who have stood by them over the years, but believe me, I know only too well that I have stood on the shoulders of giants and have at times walked in the footsteps of others.

I want to say a huge thanks to those who saw fit to nominate me, and to those who supported the nomination. Thank you for seeing something worthy enough for such an honour. Many thanks to the Leadership, past and present, of the Elim Movement, for giving me the opportunity to serve God by serving our community, and for the amazing support during some very trying years.

A very special thanks to the Leadership and everyone at New Life City Church, past and present, who have been part of this journey and are therefore rightly part of this award. To the Management Team and all our staff and volunteers at City Life Centre and Stadium Projects: this is as much your award as it is mine.

To all those within our community who are the real community workers, legitimised by your positive contributions in very difficult circumstances - thank you for what you do. You are as deserving, if not more so, of this award.

Thanks to all our many American friends and churches who have stood alongside us and encouraged us for many years and in so many ways.

Thanks also to those organisations, both statutory and private, who have strengthened our hand to be an influence for good across North and West Belfast and beyond.

A mega thanks to my son Jonathan, daughters Chara and Paula, who have stood firm in the face of some very dark and threatening days; who, like others brought up in conflict, have seen more than they ever should have seen, but have stayed the course; have been at my side and have had my back when I needed them most.

A very huge word of thanks to my wife Kathleen, because if anyone deserves an award, it's Kathleen. She has given so much to so many, and has taken on much more than she ever should have had to. No one knows better than Kathleen knows! Our story is one story.

But none of this would ever be possible without Christ. For He who called us, not only counted us faithful, but has been faithful to us. He has kept us and blessed us with a great bunch of people at New Life City Church and at City Life Centre. I with many others look forward to one day meeting with the King, and to receiving His Reward, which is far better than any earthly accolade!

Kathleen and I fully acknowledge that our visit to the Palace was an amazing moment in all of our lives. But that's all it was - a moment. That moment is now behind us, but the work we are called to do is still before us and is all around us. We continue daily to pursue together the God-given vision to reach out beyond the fish-tank to an ocean of opportunities and to a world that still has much wrong with it, yet a world that God still loves.

Buckingham Palace

Chapter 13

Our Unplanned Chapter

During the past few years, Kathleen and I have chatted back and forth about telling our story from her perspective, but with one of the main focuses being her work with children that started way back in Brown Square, leading to the launch of Hobby Horse Playgroup that Kathleen sees as her greatest achievement.

As two teenagers in love, we had no idea that our first plate of chips and two forks was the start of an amazing journey, and we had no idea of the places that we would go and the things we would do together. But we had a plan, and the plan was that what we started together, we would finish together, which is something we generally stuck to. The planning of a wedding in Belfast and a honeymoon in Portrush; the planning of a family and of raising children we would be proud of; the planning to purchase and set up a home together; the planning for Bible College, and so much more. And so, in the same way, Kathleen and I had also planned to finish this book together.

However, having faced many challenges, some of which are reflected in this book, our greatest challenge and hardest battle is the one we have been facing during the past few years – it's called Dementia. In 2016, Kathleen was diagnosed with Mild Cognitive Impairment (MCI), but things have steadily worsened in recent years. So, when Kathleen and I started out writing this book, we expected to finish it together. We've maintained this joint effort right up to the close of Chapter 12, thinking we would end the book there. So, this final chapter is entitled, 'Our Unplanned Chapter.' It includes references from Kathleen, but I now finish it by myself.

I have often said from the platform, that no one knows what others are going through. As a pastor, there have been so many times when I have felt the heartaches and the heartbreaks experienced by many due to circumstances that were beyond their control. Yet, I was often requested to keep private what they were going through, which is something I have always honoured. Others, however, were going through storms that were open for all to see, due to the nature of the problem or illness. However, maintaining privacy is something I have become good at, so there was no way I was going to detract from what anyone might be going through by drawing attention to what both Kathleen and I were experiencing.

You see, I felt I had to maintain the perception that everything was okay, even if it wasn't; I still had to act as though at least I was still in control. It didn't matter what we were going through together; it could never be about us; it was always about others. Because of this 'mindset,' I never wanted it to be about me, especially when I knew that others were in much worse situations.

Even when I was diagnosed with cancer and admitted to hospital, I was determined not to tell anyone in case the outcome was not what I had hoped and prayed for. The only person I told was Kathleen, right up until the time was near for me to go in for surgery. It was only then that I also told Jonathan what was happening, as I needed him to drive me to the hospital. The reason I did not want the focus on me, was because someone else in New Life was battling cancer. That someone was little Dempsey, who, despite every attempt by the medical profession both here and in America, and despite every effort made by her mum to save her, finally passed away in January 2017.

So, when Kathleen was diagnosed with MCI, and we were told it could very well lead to Dementia, it was not something we would broadcast, but rather we continued to take it to God in prayer, while doing everything possible to remain positive and hopeful that all would be well.

However, things have continued to decline slowly yet more noticeably, which has meant making some major decisions, and has significantly impacted on how we have lived, worked, and ministered during the past few years. Kathleen has had to take a step back from her daily routine of actively working with children, which was her life. Yet, she remains in regular contact by continuing to work with reduced responsibilities and with my input and support in helping to oversee Hobby Horse Family Project, supported very much by Paula, and with Maureen taking much more responsibility for the Playgroup, but all with my overall support. It's also meant that I've had to make some major adjustments, pulling back from an almost daily routine of meetings and travelling to minister. I also cancelled our ministry trip to the USA just before the first Covid lockdown began. Things I thought were important, no longer hold that sense of priority, not when the one I have loved since we were teenagers and who has stood faithfully by my side for over 50 years, now needs me to stand by her more than ever.

Yes, life has changed in many ways! Brown Square seems a long way off, and I know we'll never get back to some of those things we now miss. However, we remain thankful for the good days that we still enjoy together and for the many memories we can still make together as husband and wife. And we're ever so thankful for all who have stood by us and have stepped up and taken their place alongside us.

The challenge to get rid of the 'Mr Fix-it' persona, and the challenge to remove the pastoral mask, along with the projected impression that I don't need help, is still something I battle with, but it's something I am certainly prepared to acknowledge. The fact is, we all need help, as might you, the reader. I might never know your situation, but I do know in this learning curve of life that we're all going through, there are times when we all need help! And so, if you, the reader, feel you need help, I would encourage you to reach out to professional bodies, or reach out to us here at New Life City Church or to another church you might have a connection with; or in your own way just begin to reach out to God right now even as you read these words. Invite Jesus Christ to be your Lord and Saviour, and ask Him for His help and guidance. Kathleen and I have proved together over the years, as David said, that *'God is our refuge and strength, an ever-present help in times of trouble.'*[4] As I bring this book to a close, it reminds me of what Kathleen said when I asked her several years ago, when we started on this book journey together, "What would you want to say to those who have helped?"

Kathleen said:
"I deeply appreciate all the support and understanding from so many amazing people within New Life City Church and within City Life Centre, but especially those who have become not only great workers within Hobby Horse Playgroup, but more importantly, Lorraine and Maureen, who have become great friends, both of whom I love deeply. You have both been, and still are, the best ever. We have been through many highs and lows over the years, but we always got by, and we always made it together. You have done me proud in all you have achieved. Hobby Horse is as much yours as it was and is mine.

I want to thank also, the many others who have reached out to help and support me and Jackie, not just in recent times, but throughout our many years together, and in so many areas of life and ministry. We could not have made it to where we are today without your love and support."

I'll never forget the moment when Kathleen looked into my eyes and said:

"Jackie, you've been an amazing husband. We've been together and in love from when we were teenagers. I want to thank you for your support both at home and at work, and especially in recent years, but the end is not yet. We may not know what tomorrow will bring or what lies ahead, but what we do know is that the God we have served together from our early years, the same God who began a good work in us, is the same God who will one day bring it all to a glorious completion."

As I close this chapter, who knows what tomorrow really holds for any of us? But one thing we do know for sure; in the words of one of Kathleen's favourite songs, is that *'Because He lives, we can face tomorrow.'* And we can face it together. Tonight, like last night, we will be in our home. Before tomorrow comes, we'll sit and hold hands as we do each night, and we'll remember together, not only how we have loved each other, but how God has loved and blessed us as a couple and as a family in so many ways.

> *Because He lives, I can face tomorrow*
> *Because He lives, all fear is gone*
> *Because I know, I know, He holds the future*
> *And life is worth the living, just because He lives.*

Thank you to everyone who has been on this life's journey with us, but it doesn't end here!

'For our light and momentary troubles are achieving for us an eternal glory that far outweighs them all. So, we fix our eyes not on what is seen, but on what is unseen, since what is seen is temporary, but what is unseen is eternal.'

2 Corinthians 4:17-18

CONTACT DETAILS FOR

Hobby Horse Playgroup & New Life City Church
City Life Centre
143 Northumberland Street
Belfast BT13 2JF
T. 028 90239572

WEBSITES

www.HobbyHorsePlaygroup.com
www.CityLifeCentre.org

The profits from this book will be donated to Hobby Horse Playgroup.

Thank you for your purchase.

INSPIRED TO WRITE A BOOK?

Contact

Maurice Wylie Media
Your Inspirational Christian Publisher

Based in Northern Ireland and distributing around the world.
www.MauriceWylieMedia.com